new australian style

new australian style

john gollings and george michell

CHRONICLE BOOKS
SAN FRANCISCO

page 1: Philip Cox's Yulara resort at Uluru, Northern Territory
page 2: Swimmer at Yulara resort at Uluru, Northern Territory
page 5: Melbourne city skyline; Neutral Bay, Sydney; Bedarra Island, Queensland; The Olgas, Northern Territory

First published in the United States in 1999 by Chronicle Books
First published in the United Kingdom in 1999
by Thames & Hudson Ltd, London

Printed in Hong Kong

ISBN 0-8118-2544-2

Library of Congress Cataloging-in-Publication Data available.

Distributed in Canada by Raincoast Books
8680 Cambie Street, Vancouver, B.C. V6P 6M9

10 9 8 7 6 5 4 3 2 1

Chronicle Books
85 Second Street
San Francisco, CA 94105
www.chroniclebooks.com

contents

McWILLIAM
PORT
BAILEYS
Grand Marnier
COINTREAU
MALIBU
EL
TORO
GORDONS
DRY GIN
LONDON

INTRODUCTION

Australians enjoy an enviable lifestyle, with indulgent habits of entertaining, aided by an incomparable cuisine, easy access to beach and bush retreats, and frequent travel overseas. Though this picture of a privileged society may be easily discarded as idealized and unrealistic, there is some truth in the claim that a greater proportion of the nation's population has access to a wide range of leisure and cultural activities than ever before. Sport, food and wine are not the only staples of everyday life; arts festivals including theatre, opera and film are finding ever-larger audiences in almost all the major centres. Although none of these lifestyle achievements is new, there is indeed something different about Australia today. Quite simply, Australians have become visually aware: they notice their cityscapes and landscapes with unprecedented delight; they fight concertedly to preserve their historical and natural heritage; and they wish to live in houses that are not merely comfortable, but also visually challenging. This quest for an aesthetic environment underpins the new Australia style.

Most of the houses included here come from the eastern seaboard of the country, reflecting both the uneven population distribution and the concentration of design culture. The architects themselves, many of whom are still in their thirties and forties, belong to a generation that has overcome the tyranny of distance. Australians relish their place in a wider cultural world. The new Australia style is similarly global, registering most of the stylistic idioms current in Europe and the countries of the Pacific Rim. Yet the houses illustrated in this book could never have been built in Provence, Devon or California. They have a natural breezy quality, even a brashness, that is very much Australian.

Nowhere is this better seen than in the special relationship between indoors and outdoors. Like most aspects of Australian life, these new houses are outwardly focused. They open onto courts, backyards, sand dunes and bush, all the open-air settings of everyday life. Large windows, and shuttered panels or slatted openings look onto broad verandahs and continuous decks. These outdoor zones are not mere accretions, but rather extensions of the core living areas, their furthest walls, so to speak. Landscapes – a suburban garden, the nearby ocean or a surrounding forest – are fully integrated into a domestic environment that celebrates the act of gazing out. What more perfect example of this than the entrance verandah of the hilltop pavilion at Pomona in Queensland, with the Glasshouse Mountains in the distance?

Lindsay and Kerry Clare's hilltop pavilion, Pomona, Queensland

ROOTS OF THE NEW AUSTRALIA STYLE

Harry Seidler, Rose Seidler's house, Wahroonga, Sydney

The interior of Rose Seidler's house, Wahroonga, Sydney

Any survey of the last fifty years of Australian house design must inevitably focus on the careers of a number of pioneering architects. During the prosperity of the postwar years, an era marked by the rapid influx of European migrants, the building industry flourished and the suburbs of the larger cities expanded rapidly. This was the period of the mass-produced house, in particular the triple-fronted brick-veneer home which sprang up in countless versions all over the country.

It was in this economically dynamic, but aesthetically deadening, milieu that Harry Seidler and Roy Grounds became active. Thanks mainly to these two figures, Australian design was brought into line with the mainstream modernist movement that had already affected Europe and the United States. Seidler's glass and whitewashed, reinforced concrete houses built in Sydney in the late forties and fifties were startling for their clean lines, unfussy detailing and dramatically cantilevered volumes. Grounds preferred wood and glass, and his houses in and around Melbourne during the same period are intimate, inward-looking projects. Both architects were interested in simple geometric forms which they juxtaposed effectively with the natural settings of suburban and bush sites.

The sixties ushered in a new generation of designers, such as Peter Muller, Bruce Rickard and Ken Woolley in Sydney, and Robin Boyd and Alistair Knox in Melbourne. Remaining faithful to the newly established modernist principles, they began to explore what was perceived at the time as a more authentically Australian idiom. This was expressed in the conscientious integration of houses into their settings, and in the deliberate choice of inexpensive natural materials, like timber frames and floors, clinker brick walls and sloping tiled roofs. Low cost and practicality were guiding principles, and indeed most of these houses were modest in scale and unpretentious in spirit.

It was not until the seventies that Australian domestic design achieved the aesthetic breakthrough that was to affect so much later work. This may be explained partly by the favourable economic climate of the times, and partly by the fact that Australians had become less concerned with national identity and were feeling more at ease with an internationalist view of their place in the world. The most celebrated architect to emerge during this decade was Glenn Murcutt, whose minimalist, lightweight metallic structures attracted considerable attention. To Murcutt must be credited the notion of transforming the corrugated iron bush shed into an elegant and comfortable house that adhered to modernist ideals. While Murcutt was by no means the only practitioner to explore such architectural transmutations, his work attained the most renown and was widely imitated.

The seventies and early eighties were also inventive years for other designers. Richard LePlaistrier, for instance, continued to develop the vernacular idiom of the sixties, creating delicately detailed wooden houses that were sensitively integrated into their forested sites north of Sydney. Philip Cox took a different approach, specializing in sail-like tension structures which could be adapted to a variety of uses, such as his resort at Uluru in the central Australian desert. Meanwhile, in Victoria, Daryl Jackson and Gregory Burgess were extending the possibilities of timber-framed construction by fashioning boldly angled wall planes, projecting balconies and towered outlooks. This somewhat determined, expressionistic approach was further developed in the work of Edmond and Corrigan, whose houses made self-conscious allusions to the suburban vernacular in which they were set. This referential manner marked the beginning of the postmodern fashion that was enthusiastically taken up by some of the Melbourne designers. These practitioners had some success in adapting this style to the solid masonry construction suited to the coolest of Australia's mainland cities. However, the striking expressionistic possibilities of postmodernism were not to be fully realized until the nineties.

Roy Grounds house, Mount Martha, Victoria

Alistair Knox's house in Eltham, Victoria

Domestic building in the warmer subtropical zones of the country only became innovative during the eighties. Under such trailblazers as Gabriel Poole, a new Queensland school was born, drawing its inspiration from a long-standing vernacular tradition. Climate has strongly influenced the design of Queensland houses, whose rooms often open out onto balconies encased in wooden screens or canvas awnings. While the boom that transformed Queensland's undeveloped beaches into world-famous holiday destinations was doubtless responsible for the resurgence of building activity in the region, it was the enterprise of Poole and his followers that forged a distinctive regional style. Many of the houses built in and around Brisbane at this time married the tin fabric of the outback shack with the slatted verandahs and overhanging roofs of the historic vernacular 'Queenslander'.

While this rapid survey hardly does justice to the talents and enterprise of the many designers who have populated the Australian architectural scene since mid-century, it does give some idea of the fertile relationships that developed between indigenous traditions, some harking back to earlier times, and newly imported ideas. All of these tendencies converge in Australia's current domestic design, the diversity of which reflects the unbridled energies of a younger generation of practitioners. If no single idiom prevails, this is because the new Australia style is essentially pluralistic: hardly surprising in a society which prides itself on the variety of its cultural influences.

Ed Lippmann's house in Mosman, Sydney

Engelen Moore's house in Neutral Bay, Sydney

Bob Nation's Fitzroy apartment, Melbourne

opposite Andrew Nolan's extension to a Victorian house, Paddington, Sydney

LATE MODERNIST ELEGANCE

Australia's ties with global design movements are best seen in the varieties of modernism that have flourished there in recent decades. Late modernism continues to delight in the open planning, clean lines and preference for timber, glass and whitewashed masonry that had already gained currency in mid-century. In the hands of the most experienced Sydney architects, these attributes achieve a smooth elegance, as can be seen in the houses of Alex Popov, Ed Lippmann and Alexander Tzannes, or the apartments of Neil Durbach and Burley Katon Halliday. Sydney's fascination with late modernism is partly explained by the harbourside sites of many of these projects, the restrained visual content of this idiom providing a perfect foil to the brilliance of water and sky. Even when a water view is not available, as in Andrew Nolan's immaculate extension to a Victorian house in Paddington, the late modernist aesthetic prevails. The newly designed living-kitchen area of this project juxtaposes stone tiles, whitewashed walls and warmly toned timber surfaces according to a rigorous but homely formalism.

Some Sydney practitioners, not content with the comfortable qualities of late modernism, have evolved a more demanding minimalist style. In their various houses, the architects Engelen Moore strip down interiors to the barest essentials, leaving only unadorned white walls and ceilings, with, inevitably, white-on-white furniture and fittings. Other Sydney practitioners invest late modernism with a greater drama, nowhere better seen than in Renato D'Ettore's remarkable clifftop palazzo at Coogee. This house endorses the open planning and symmetrical layouts of late modernism, but adds a wider range of materials to achieve a striking visual richness.

Late modernism also makes an appearance in and around Melbourne, but here a sterner aspect of the style is expressed. The interior of Barrie Marshall's beach house is dominated by untreated concrete walls, polished blackened floors, galvanized iron room-dividers and pivoting doors. A similar range of industrially derived surfaces is employed by the architect Allan Powell for his various projects. Bob Nation's ingenious warehouse conversion is lighter in spirit, though no less rigid in its use of metallic trusses, greenish glass panels and whitewashed fittings. Sean Godsell sustains this metallic approach by encasing the typically modernist glazed living space of a new house for himself in a filigree of rusting steel.

Ranging from smooth elegance to tough minimalism, the late modernist tendencies of the new Australia style effectively encompass a broad range of expressions. This no doubt explains its increasing popularity among designers and clients.

POSTMODERNIST WIT

Postmodernism developed in parallel to late modernism, and is characterized by a more liberal approach to architectural volumes, shapes and materials. A typical feature of Australian late postmodernism is a witty approach to colour, such as that exhibited with considerable panache by the architect Geoff Lovie. His bright purple and box-like timber-clad house is enhanced by yellow window frames and cut-out verandahs. Colour is handled with equal flair by Andrew Metcalf who takes delight in contrasting curving glass panes and glass brick walls with brightly painted steel girders.

A dynamic version of postmodernism is seen in the recent work of several Melbourne designers. Kai Chen and Tom Kovac ignore the constraints of the right angle in order to permit curving arcs of masonry to sweep around and into their houses. Living and sleeping areas in these projects take on an almost hallucinatory character, with subtle lighting emphasizing the fluidity of walls and ceilings. These tendencies reach their climax in the work of Ivan Rijavec, whose houses exhibit curving and angled planes pierced by differently shaped windows to dizzying effect. The interior of his Templestowe house, for instance, is enhanced by lilac and bottle-green wall surfaces and tear-shaped skylights with blue and yellow sides.

Other exponents of postmodernism in Melbourne are committed to a tougher, more expressionistic style, often with cantilevered volumes and spiky contrasts of texture. Superimposed living and sleeping zones in Dale Jones-Evans's postmodern dwelling are walled with sloping masonry buttresses, weatherboard cladding and diamond-shaped zinc tiles. The upper bedroom juts out cheekily over an ornamental pond. A family villa designed by the architects Wood Marsh articulates different zones by exaggerating the junctions between them. This device is also pursued by Nonda Katsalidis, whose oceanside bunker presents an arresting dissimilarity of rusting iron and weathered timber surfaces.

All of these traits are manifest in the work of the Melbourne architects Denton Corker Marshall, a firm which has by now achieved a distinctive postmodern personality. Nowhere is this better seen than in the brightly painted, metallic surfaces and witty textural contrasts of the lobby, restaurant, rooftop pool and bar, and bedrooms of the Adelphi Hotel. While these angular and colouristic features may at first seem to represent a somewhat idiosyncratic brand of postmodernism, they are in fact an increasingly familiar feature of the more public expressions of the new Australia style.

opposite Ivan Rijavec's Templestowe house, Melbourne

Geoff Lovie's timber-clad house, Queanbeyan

Tom Kovac's restaurant, Tonic, in Darlinghurst, Sydney

Denton Corker Marshall's Adelphi Hotel, Melbourne

SHEDS AND SHACKS

Beverley Garlick's country retreat in New South Wales

Gabriel Poole's triple-shed house in Queensland

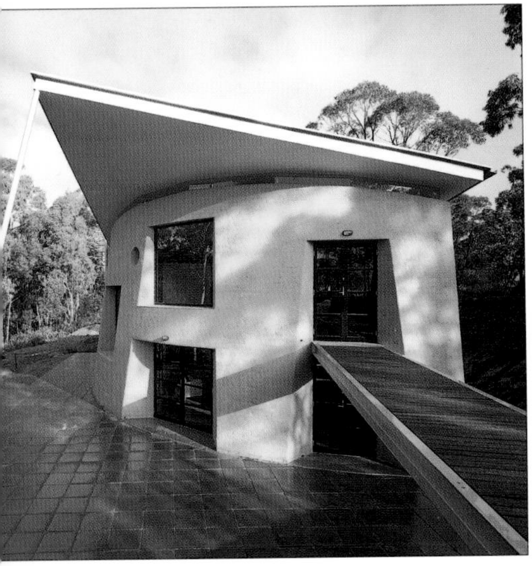

Grose Bradley's weekend house in South Australia

Some designers have rejected modernism and postmodernism altogether in their quest for an authentic Australian idiom, turning instead to the vernacular bush shed or beach shack. These unpretentious structures have a long history in Australian building practice, but they have only recently been upgraded into élite residences. While this transformation may be dismissed as urban nostalgia for a lost rural lifestyle, it has nevertheless been responsible for some remarkable architectural innovations.

The typical Australian metallic-shed house is laid out as a simple rectangle, with a living-dining-kitchen area in the middle and bedrooms and bathroom at one or both ends. The houses are constructed with a simple wooden frame, with walls often made of plywood, and corrugated iron reserved for the angled or gabled roof. The interior is spare, with the supporting frame clearly visible between the inexpensive materials that coat the walls and ceiling. Such a scheme is respected by Beverley Garlick in her country retreat in outback New South Wales. This residential complex consists of a group of elementary structures roofed with 'barrel vaults' of corrugated iron. Plywood panelling sustains the rural quality of the interiors, as do the rudimentary finishes of the kitchen and bathroom. Gabriel Poole's own dwelling near Lake Weyba in Queensland consists of a trio of sheds, each facing the back of the other, linked by a covered walkway flanked by water tanks. This multiplication of the shed elements permits an unusual spatial separation of living-dining, bathing and sleeping areas. Poole softens the overall metallic effect by stretching translucent vinyl sheeting over the steel trusses and introducing brightly coloured panels into the walls. Lindsay Holland combines a trio of metallic sheds in a completely different manner to achieve a spacious U-shaped plan for his country homestead in Victoria. Corrugated cladding runs smoothly up the walls to join the angled and curved roofing of the shed-like wings; it even invades the interior to create an enveloping metallic environment suitable for both living and sleeping.

That the shed prototype is capable of a forceful, industrial aesthetic is demonstrated by the architects Grose Bradley. The jagged metallic frame of their house at Balgownie south of Sydney dominates both the inside and the outside, with factory-like vents protruding from the gabled roof over the central living-dining space. In a weekend house by the same architects in the Adelaide Hills, South Australia, the use of metal is confined to a canopy extending beyond the building's mud-brick core. In their addition to a grandiose family mansion in Melbourne, the architects Glenn Murcutt and Robert Bruce converted the rural metallic paradigm into a luxurious suburban residence. The double-height living room benefits from a seamless wall of glass with bronze-tinted glass panels pivoting outwards from an intricately detailed steel frame.

The metamorphosis of the beach shack, clad in painted fibro-cement or plywood, is no less remarkable than that of the metallic shed. In John Mainwaring's own residence on the Sunshine Coast in Queensland, the shack is turned into a comfortable house topped with a lightweight, sinuously curving metallic canopy. Bud Brannigan's own house in suburban Brisbane recalls the shack archetype by retaining plywood cladding throughout. The living-dining balcony that forms the nucleus of this design is best understood as a suburban variant of the beach-house deck. In his towered cabin on Phillip Island in Victoria, Peter Maddison returns to the modest scale and materials of the original. Aesthetic interest here is achieved through an articulated timber frame that angles outwards from the fibro-panelled walls to serve as both a balcony and a sun shield.

John Mainwaring's house in Queensland

Closely related to the shed-shack concept is the pavilion house, often no more than an open wooden or metal structure topped with a gabled roof. Glenn Murcutt's pavilion studio in Arnhem Land achieves an exceptional airiness due to its use of plywood panels angled outwards to trap the breeze. The securely fixed timbers of the structural frame and the total absence of glass are essential in this part of the Northern Territory where cyclones are common. The pavilion format is also well suited to temperate settings, as is shown by the simply constructed forest cabin designed and partly built by the architect Peter Stuchbury in a eucalyptus grove above Pittwater, an hour north of Sydney. This project consists of superimposed living-cooking and sleeping zones roofed by an arc of corrugated iron; sliding panels open up the interior to the surrounding forest, while dining takes place on an extended wooden deck sheltered by a canopy.

Bud Brannigan's plywood house in Brisbane

Transparency of texture is also a particular feature of the Queensland species of pavilion house. The Stradbroke Island holiday retreat of Brit Andresen and Peter O'Gorman is laid out in a long double-height rectangle incorporating an interior sandy court planted with trees. Clad in slatted timbers, shuttered panels and glass, there is no clear distinction between indoors and outdoors, an impression reinforced by the living-dining belvedere that projects outwards from the front of the house. Another quite different version of the slatted pavilion house is Gerard Murtagh's bunker-like weekender at Sunshine Beach, Queensland, which has closed-in decks with shuttered openings through which the Pacific can be glimpsed.

Such transformations of the basic shed and shack, whether in beach or bush settings, give full expression to the imaginative dimension of the new Australia style. They testify to a creativity and versatility barely detectable in earlier times.

Brit Andresen and Peter O'Gorman's open-webbed house on Stradbroke Island, Queensland

EXIT
today

Harry Seidler's duplex overlooking Sydney harbour

CITY

Angelo Candalepas's apartment project, Pyrmont, Sydney

Although Australia might still seem a young country, the formative phase of the nation's history took place over a hundred years ago in the nineteenth century. A substantial architectural record survives from this time, as may be seen in the Victorian cores of the major cities, some of which, like Adelaide and Melbourne, were laid out on expandable grids. These inner-city zones are dotted with grandiose civic monuments, many now restored. They are also crowded with factories and warehouses, not to mention handsome row houses with cast iron balconies, as in Sydney's Paddington or Melbourne's South Yarra. These industrial and residential relics are now much sought after as desirable dwellings by Australians keen to rediscover the virtues of city life. This process has accelerated in recent years, leading to a rapid revitalization of inner urban environments and the construction of new projects, such as the densely packed apartment scheme by Angelo Candalepas in Sydney's crowded Pyrmont district.

Building in the historical locales of cities imposes severe restrictions upon architects, but many have responded creatively to the challenge by adapting older properties to late twentieth-century expectations. A popular solution for many householders is to leave intact the outer brick shells of their recently acquired factories and houses, and to remodel the interiors. A striking example of this trend is Bob Nation's warehouse conversion whose interior was gutted in order to create an industrial-style apartment in Melbourne's Fitzroy. Nation overcomes the problems of space limitation by reducing the kitchen and bathroom areas to functional annexes, and creating free-standing cupboards with multiple doors to serve as room-dividers. The result is a late modernist steel-and-glass fantasy that completely belies the original dilapidated and brick-faced exterior. Another Fitzroy project, a factory house by the architect Ivan Rijavec, is more fanciful. The space inside an old factory has been imaginatively transformed into a two-storey family home. The modest scale of the interior is offset by the curve of the free-standing chimney shaft which sweeps upward without interruption. This gives the enclosed space a dynamic quality that contrasts with the rigid brick box inside which it is contained. Such warped surfaces and spatial complexities are typical of Rijavec's highly individual brand of postmodernism.

Another example of architectural improvisation within a nineteenth-century urban environment is a design by Nonda Katsalidis. Building outwards from an abandoned cluster of grain silos in Richmond, Katsalidis has fashioned a sequence of apartments with prows of rusting iron that survey the changing industrial landscape of this inner Melbourne zone. A less ambitious approach to the problems of accommodating a late twentieth-century lifestyle within an earlier fabric has been developed by the architectural firm of Neometro. Their adaptation of a warehouse in Melbourne's St Kilda is a lesson in minimal costs and aesthetic restraint. One studio apartment in this revamped building is little more than a refurbishment of the existing industrial space, with a simple kitchen bench and bathroom annex fitted into one corner. There is no actual bedroom, the sleeping zone being defined by a curtain that is merely pulled out when required.

Opportunities to build anew in the inner cities are rare and eagerly sought after by architects and their clients. The late modernist studio residence in Redfern designed by the architects Engelen Moore stands in a typical nineteenth-century inner-city area of Sydney. The façade of the building is a white-washed concrete grid with metallic slatted infills which perfectly matches the proportions of its Victorian neighbours. It is a surprise to enter and discover a virtually vacant box, with only token signs of habitation. The effect of emptiness is

Downtown Melbourne

The Melbourne skyline

The Adelphi Hotel surrounded by Melbourne's Victorian buildings

accentuated by the radical device of opening up the rear of the house from floor to ceiling, permitting the interior space to flow outwards into a back court with a pond shadowed by a spreading tree. The kitchen is reduced to a mere workbench, while the bedroom and the glazed chamber that serves as the bathroom occupy a mezzanine.

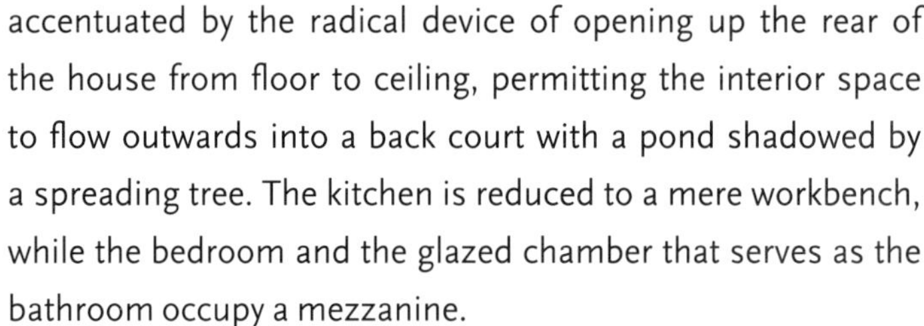

Some designers demonstrate great ingenuity in juxtaposing new and old. Neil Durbach and Camilla Block's rooftop apartment in Surry Hills, another of Sydney's inner-city zones, stands on top of an older building with no attempt at visual homogeneity. The outer walls of the apartment curve provocatively but usefully to create a sheltered outdoor terrace. This curve contrasts with the cubic form of the older supporting brick structure, a differentiation that is reinforced by the use of zinc sheets to cloak the exterior surfaces. The curving wall continues on the inside of the apartment, giving the elongated living-dining space a unique spatial fluidity. Andrew Nolan is less assertive in his juxtaposition of new and old, as may be seen from his subtle additions to a typical nineteenth-century house in a quiet Paddington street. The elegant living-dining-kitchen extension is surrounded by polished wood surfaces and sliding glass walls that permit the interior to open up entirely. The swimming pool in the outer court connects the house to a guest wing built against the rear wall of the property.

Not all new residential structures in the inner cities are concerned to blend in with their older architectural surroundings. The animated façades of Nonda Katsalidis's apartment block in the middle of Melbourne completely ignore the nearby late nineteenth-century Victoria Market. Instead, they present an unlikely combination of classically inspired bronze reliefs and postmodern concrete frames and metallic balconies. The block is notable for its severely minimalist interiors, one of which was commissioned by a graphic designer who insisted on the sparest decor for his living-dining space, library and bedroom. In another recently completed high-rise in Melbourne's centre, Katsalidis shows his ability to manipulate steel and glass. The luxurious duplex that crowns this building is flooded with light that enters through floor-to-ceiling windows shielded by metallic louvres.

The work of the architects Burley Katon Halliday expresses a lyrical elegance that characterizes the best of Sydney's designers. Their harbourside apartment at Elizabeth Bay employs full-height windows and a curving glass balcony to guarantee unimpeded views of the harbour immediately in

Cafés at Southbank in Melbourne

Surfer's Paradise in Queensland, high-rise development on the Pacific

front. The interior employs polished marble floors, smoothly stuccoed walls and imaginatively placed lighting, the hallmarks of Sydney late modernism. The virtually colourless interior is a perfect foil to the brilliant water and sky whose reflections pervade the interior. All these attributes are often found in the buildings of Sydney's most famous architect, Harry Seidler. His duplex on the topmost floors of a newly completed multi-storeyed complex at Milsons Point serves as a residential appendage to a busy architectural office. Undulating glass walls opening onto continuous balconies offer a magnificent panorama of the harbour bridge and the city beyond. The dramatically twisting staircase rising from the central lobby-living space is a focal point for the sparsely furnished interior.

Lifestyle design opportunities in the inner cities extend beyond urban dwellings, and Australians clearly relish the joys of socializing in public. If designers have on occasion been restrained in the interiors that they have fashioned for clients at home, they have certainly been encouraged to extend their imagination when out and about. Restaurants, bars and clubs with ever more idiosyncratic interiors are opening all the time in Sydney and Melbourne, demonstrating that culinary explorations can be accompanied by aesthetic adventures.

Designs for new hotels and revamped older accommodation in the inner cities are equally imaginative. A fine example is the Prince of Wales Hotel in St Kilda, one of Melbourne's most animated night-time locales. Allan Powell has infused this stodgy Art Deco building with a new elegance, juxtaposing timber and dark masonry textures with brightly coloured fabrics. The result is a set of comfortable but sophisticated low-key interiors. A more exuberant project is the unashamedly postmodern Adelphi Hotel which the architects Denton Corker Marshall have fashioned out of the carcass of a disused warehouse in the middle of Melbourne's inner city. The angled steel surfaces and vivid colours of the lobby announce the jaunty character of this fashionable place, an aesthetic that is sustained in some of the rooms. The basement restaurant is more restrained, in contrast to the brightly painted rooftop bar which overlooks a narrow lap pool audaciously jutting out beyond the building line.

Whether for outdoor or indoor living, all of these projects demonstrate the ability of Australian designers to work within older urban environments, while fully exploring the aesthetic potential of late modernism and postmodernism.

FACTORY HOUSE, FITZROY, MELBOURNE

radical transformations

In his transformation of a small factory in the Fitzroy district of Melbourne, the architect Ivan Rijavec gutted the interior to create a double-height family home. The living-dining space is dominated by a fireplace with a narrow chimney shaft that curves boldly upwards where it is lit by porthole lights set into the ceiling. This shaft liberates the house from its cubical brick shell, contributing to the overall dynamic quality of the interior. Similar curves are used for the staircase that ascends to the gallery and bedrooms. Even the Pepe chairs around the fireplace are curved!

above The kitchen set into one corner of the house

right The fireplace and its curving chimney shaft form the core of the house

opposite above A small covered balcony projects outwards from the original brick walls of the factory

opposite below The chairs around the fireplace echo the curves of the ceiling

above Sharp-edged balustrades at the top of the staircase

left The bedroom showing the brightly painted circular skylights

opposite The living-dining area is overlooked by the upper gallery

white on white

Commissioned by a photographer who wished to combine his residence and studio, the architects Engelen Moore conceived this house in a severely minimalist style. The interior details are pared down, the living and sleeping zones being reduced to a single double-height space completely devoid of detail. The white-on-white colour scheme is sustained throughout, especially in the sofa and kitchen bench which were designed by the architects.

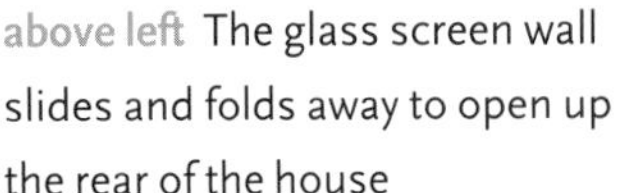

above left The glass screen wall slides and folds away to open up the rear of the house

above right The rear of the house with its glass screen wall looking out to a small garden

right The structural grid and metallic louvres of the exterior harmonize with the lines of the Victorian houses in this inner-city Sydney street

above The central living area has a kitchen bench at the rear; a mezzanine gallery above serves as a bedroom with a bathroom and studio beyond

right The glass shower cubicle positioned beneath a skylight

DUPLEX, MELBOURNE CITY

louvred luxury

Occupying the two uppermost levels of a high-rise office building, this boldly designed apartment is intended for sophisticated urban living. While the architect Nonda Katsalidis has done little to conceal the supporting steel frame of the building inside the living-dining area, he offsets the solidity of the metallic effect by a liberal use of glass with louvred shades. The result is an interior flooded with streaked light.

above A flight of steps to the rear of the seating area ascends to the bedrooms on the upper level

left Seating is focused on a colourful rug laid out in front of a wood-burning stove

opposite above The duplex is set among the high-rise buildings of Melbourne's inner city

opposite below Double-height windows with metallic louvres afford the living area a splendid vista of Melbourne's skyline

ARTIST'S STUDIO, BRUNSWICK, MELBOURNE

low-cost living

Commissioned by a young photographic artist, this studio was fashioned out of the lofty roof space of the old Brunswick food market. A living-dining area forms the core, with a small kitchen to one side, from which a ladder ascends to a study. A darkroom and bathroom are tucked into the space beside the far staircase which ascends to the bedrooms. The architect Geoff Crosby has used the simplest materials throughout, not only to save expense but also to create an ingenious and efficient living-working space.

opposite above The refurbished 1920s Brunswick market that now houses artists' studios

opposite Even the space below the stairs is utilized for living and working

above The densely packed interior. A ladder leads to a mezzanine bedroom and a study

lustrous elegance

Overlooking the water from one of Sydney's innermost harbourside locations, this spacious apartment is typical of the late modernist manner advocated by the designers Burley Katon Halliday. Transparency and lightness are the prevailing qualities of the living-dining area, with its unframed floor-to-ceiling windows and whitewashed walls. Polished marble floors and the occasional steel surface or Thai silk panel guarantee an atmosphere of lustrous elegance.

opposite above The cleverly curving balcony of the apartment, shielded by an almost invisible waist-high glass guard, optimizes the panoramic views of Sydney harbour

opposite below Enlarged photographs by Tracey Moffat animate the corridor leading to the suite of four bedrooms

right Shuttered windows line the street, providing the apartment with essential privacy

below Furnished for formal living, the living-dining area looks out over the harbour

top left Cooking takes place in a stainless-steel niche at one end of the kitchen

top right Marble steps lead to the sunken tub in the luxuriously appointed bathroom

above White bed covers and translucent white curtains soften the bedroom interior

right A mirrored wall and a shallow floor pool transform the stair well into a delight of reflecting surfaces

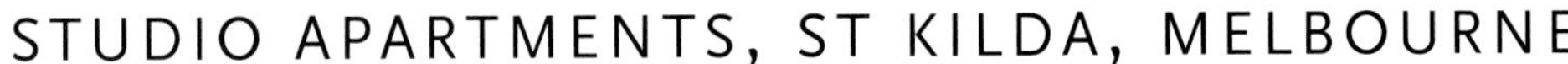

STUDIO APARTMENTS, ST KILDA, MELBOURNE

back to basics

Occupying a remodelled industrial warehouse in Melbourne's St Kilda, these studios are an exercise in basic living. The architects Neometro have merely scrubbed the concrete floor and whitewashed the existing walls and ceiling, leaving the furniture and fittings to the occupants. In one apartment, living and dining takes place in a single open space, the kitchen being reduced to a stainless steel bench placed against one wall. A simple curtain defines the sleeping corner.

top The warehouse with its reworked street façade and double-storey rooftop addition

above The kitchen bench, white plastic bathroom panels and curtained sleeping area in one of the apartments

right This kitchen makes much use of stainless steel

opposite The kitchen-living area of the duplex

prow-like balconies

This project by Nonda Katsalidis is a striking addition to the industrial landscape of one of Melbourne's inner-city zones. Extending outwards from a clover-leaf formation of four disused grain silos, the design has created a sequence of superimposed apartments, each with a prow-like balcony of rusting iron. The same material was used to fashion the open grille that overhangs the street elevation, thereby finishing the building off with a melodramatic flourish.

above left The pointed balconies of the apartments give the building an unusual ship-like appearance

above right The apartments are surrounded by restored industrial buildings

left Curving windows contain the living space of the penthouse, offering views in all directions

right A cheekily undulating chest of drawers in the bedroom

a minimalist vision of steel and glass

Bob Nation's conversion of a small warehouse in the inner Melbourne suburb of Fitzroy is a model of contrasts. Leaving the outer shell of the building in its original derelict condition, Nation transforms the interior into a minimalist vision of steel and glass. The living area is a single large space, with a cupboard-like kitchen flanked by glazed bedroom and bathroom annexes. Free-standing storage blocks open up ingeniously to serve as room-dividers. All other furniture is reduced to a minimum.

above The untouched gabled brick façade gives little hint of the interior

right A space-saving, folding storage block opens like a piece of sculpture

far right The kitchen area to one side contains an industrial-style bench; a sliding glass panel leads to the bedroom

ROOFTOP APARTMENT, SURRY HILLS, SYDNEY

urban refuge

In their design for an apartment rising above the skyline of Surry Hills, one of Sydney's innermost zones, Neil Durbach and Camilla Block made little attempt to blend in with the older supporting brick building. The rooftop extension comprises a long double-height living-dining space, from which a staircase winds upwards to the mezzanine bedroom and bath at one end. The warm-toned wooden finishes of the interior complement with the gleaming zinc sheets which clad the outer walls, giving the apartment a welcoming, inward-looking quality which contrasts with its high-level views across the city.

opposite above The zinc-clad wall creates an outdoor seating area

opposite below The double-height glazed end of the apartment is a conspicuous addition to the skyline

right Looking down on the living-dining space from the mezzanine bedroom

below Inside, the curved wall transforms the living-dining area into a long, sinuous space

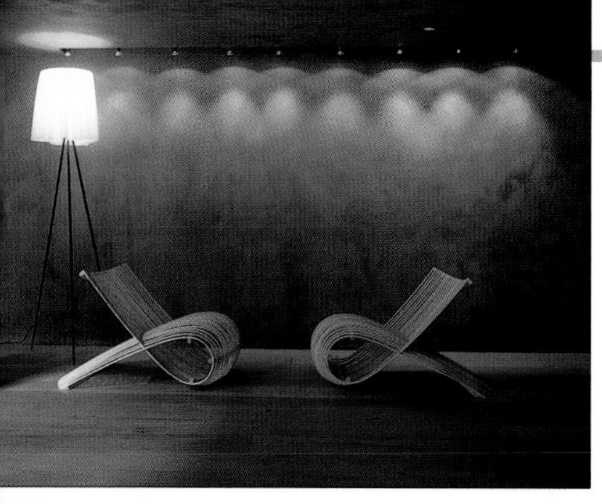

PRINCE OF WALES HOTEL, ST KILDA, MELBOURNE

mid-century revival

In his refurbishment of this landmark hotel, the architect Allan Powell departs from a strictly conservationist approach in order to create an imaginative, mid-century ambience. This has been achieved through a subtle handling of colours and textures, and the use of large areas of glass wherever possible. The hotel and its sophisticated clientele have contributed to the revitalization of this animated beachside resort within Melbourne's inner city.

far left The private dining room which opens onto an inner court has a fireplace at one end set into stucco walls, flanked by panels of coloured fabric

left A traditional tub in one of the hotel's bathrooms

below One of the bedrooms, with its brightly toned furniture and wall panels

opposite above Bent-plywood chairs in the lobby announce the low-key but refined aesthetic of the hotel

opposite below The restaurant on the first floor is an exercise in subdued elegance, with white leather furniture, suspended wicker lamps and silk drapes

outer exuberance, inner calm

This residential block in Melbourne's inner city is a showpiece for the exuberant brand of postmodernism that characterizes the work of Nonda Katsalidis. Classical references abound at the moulded metallic entrances to the building, in contrast to the boldly articulated concrete frame which rises above. Commissioned by a graphic designer, this duplex apartment is an austere exercise in minimalist living, with only the barest surfaces, fittings and furnishings.

above The street façade is topped with pairs of corrugated concrete fins

left A wall of bookshelves and a dramatically curving lamp in the study

above The doors at street level are flanked by bronze panels embossed with figures taken from classical mythology. The head of the centaur at the entrance (opposite above) portrays the developer of the building

below Fully exposed concrete structural elements dominate the living-dining area

above The bathroom features a granite bench with a stainless steel cover which eliminates the traditional handbasin

left An austere concrete staircase with a minimalist handrail

harbourside entertaining

This spacious apartment, adjoining the office of the architect Harry Seidler, is intended for formal entertaining and out-of-town guests rather than for everyday living. The duplex has long balconies with undulating glass guards on both levels, affording matchless views of the harbour. The reception-dining areas are on the lower level, with a living space and a study bedroom above. The marble floors, stairway treads and table-tops contrast with the stark whiteness of the walls and ceilings.

above left The view of the harbour bridge and city beyond from the lower balcony

left The living area with a glass wall giving onto the upper balcony

above and opposite below The twisting staircase dominates the lower level, separating the lobby from the dining area; the painted wooden sculpture on the side wall is by Frank Stella

opposite above Looking down on the lobby from the living area

inner-city panache

Denton Corker Marshall show considerable panache in their transformation of a disused factory in the heart of Melbourne. The Adelphi Hotel adds a stylish note to the inner city, being a combination of residence, restaurant, bar and private club. Although they retained as much as possible of the masonry fabric of the original building, the architects have not hesitated to add brightly coloured steel panels, struts and canopies to create the lively ambience for which the hotel is renowned.

left The hotel from the street, showing the original façade

opposite left A two-storey health club and bar are sited at the end of the rooftop swimming pool

opposite right The pool runs for much of the length of the building, protruding audaciously over the parapet

below The reception area of the restaurant is flanked by a wall of stainless steel

right The seating area before the restaurant

far right Bright colours and cheekily angled metal and leather furniture animate the lobby

below One of the bedrooms with its metallic furniture

opening up the interior

Andrew Nolan's imaginative extension to a narrow Victorian house in Sydney's Paddington is conceived as a series of contrasts between polished wooden surfaces, black leather furniture and luxurious planting. The living-dining area, which incorporates a miniature internal garden, has sliding glass doors opening onto an outer court dominated by a lap pool. The pool is entered by diving under a small cascade that issues from a guest wing built up against the rear wall.

above The glass wall in the upper bedroom overlooks the internal garden

right Sliding glass panes open to give access to the garden

left View of the house extension from the roof of the guest wing

below The built-in dining table and the pool and small cascade beyond seem to occupy the same space, thanks to the subtle use of sliding glass panels

Melbourne's eastern suburbs from the air

SUBURB

SUBURB

Most Australians live in suburbs with featureless streets laid out in ever-expanding grids. The houses are inevitably undistinguished, and only too often repetitive. But this environment, though monotonous, need not be devoid of charm, as can be seen in Sydney's harbourside suburbs, such as Neutral Bay or Mosman with their villas poised over the water, or in Melbourne's eastern suburbs, such as Toorak and Kew with their leafy streets and grandiose mansions. That not all home owners have succumbed to aesthetic conformity is borne out by a number of innovative projects. Turning their backs on their neighbours to create a private world, even on occasion disregarding the decorum of the street, these new houses are witness to a truly independent spirit intent upon discovering the creative possibilities of suburban life.

What then is the typical Australian suburban house? While various architectural idioms exist side by side in the outer realms of Sydney, Melbourne, Brisbane and Perth, these stylistic variations mask a fairly standardized strategy. At the core of almost all suburban homes is an extended living space that serves as the hub of all domestic activities: cooking, dining, supervising children, viewing television, reading newspapers, surfing the net. As householders advance financially and socially, this hallowed locus of family life tends to expand until it almost overwhelms the interior. Invariably glazed and timber-floored, the living zone opens readily onto the deck and garden beyond, both of which are intended as open-air extensions of the interior. Sleeping areas may once have been treated as secondary spaces, but these days Australians have developed an appetite for capacious bedrooms with walk-in closets and lavishly appointed en-suite bathrooms.

Houses in Paddington, Sydney

Given the all-pervasiveness of such houses across the country, it is a relief to come across fresh projects like the architect Geoff Lovie's own timber-clad house in Queanbeyan, just outside Canberra. Ignoring the well-behaved surroundings of his mundane suburban street, Lovie presents a bright purple façade punctuated by yellow window frames and balconies. Inside, however, the house is more discreet. The living-dining area that occupies the upper level has a natural timber floor and kitchen bench, with whitewashed walls and ceiling. Other approaches to domestic interiors are more courageous. Ivan Rijavec's house with curves in Templestowe, one of Melbourne's sprawling eastern suburbs, has a twisting staircase that ascends to the living space, arriving at an elliptical-shaped service core framed by sloping walls. The exterior of this house is equally daring, with its changing sequences of curving and coloured walls that completely disregard the architectural monochrome of the suburban setting. A similar preference for arcs of masonry is detectable in Tom Kovac's whitewashed moulded house in nearby Hawthorn. But here all colour is abandoned, with invariable white-on-white surfaces to emphasize the curvaceous geometry of the architecture. These bending walls invade the interior to wrap around the core living-dining area, thereby unifying inside and outside.

Recent work in Brisbane illustrates a quite different, but no less ingenious, treatment of the suburban model. Architects active in and around the city have turned the basic domestic scheme inside out, so that the nucleus of the house becomes a partially outdoor space. A simple demonstration of this architectural reversal is seen in Bud Brannigan's plywood house in St Lucia. Here the main level is built around an extended balcony-living area placed between the kitchen and interior living room. Plywood panels and suspended wooden louvres refer to the Queensland vernacular tradition, helping the house to blend in with its neighbours. The idea of an outdoor living room is taken further by the architects Donovan Hill in

Alex Popov's multiple pavilion house in Neutral Bay, Sydney

Alexander Tzannes's masonry villa in Bellevue Hill, Sydney

Neutral Bay, Sydney

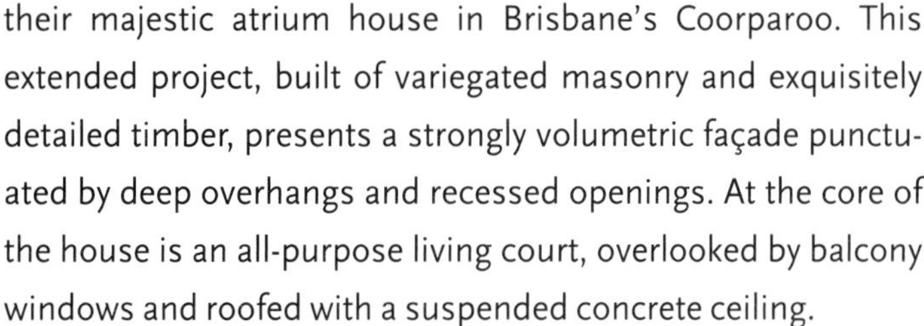

their majestic atrium house in Brisbane's Coorparoo. This extended project, built of variegated masonry and exquisitely detailed timber, presents a strongly volumetric façade punctuated by deep overhangs and recessed openings. At the core of the house is an all-purpose living court, overlooked by balcony windows and roofed with a suspended concrete ceiling.

Some Melbourne designers have evolved their own distinctive postmodern approach. Dale Jones-Evans imbues his Hawthorn dwelling with an unusual vibrancy, using angled walls, deeply set windows, cantilevered timbered overhangs and zinc shingles. Inside, a flying wooden gallery links the upper sleeping zones, removing the need for the more usual corridor. Windows at floor level permit glimpses of a densely planted garden on one side. Wood Marsh's family villa in Caulfield is more severe, confronting the street with a forbidding ellipse of concrete with an enigmatic mirrored glass cube protruding outwards. After passing through the lobby, empty except for a theatrical steel-panelled staircase that ascends to the master bedroom, the visitor arrives at the living room with its wall of glass opening onto a private garden.

Sydney's new suburban design is distinguished by a distilled version of late modernism, whose preferred materials are whitewashed masonry and large expanses of glazing with occasional touches of silvered metal and polished timber. The suitability of this lightweight, low-key aesthetic for suburban projects with harbour views is demonstrated by Alex Popov in his multiple pavilion house in Neutral Bay. Living and dining areas here open onto courts and a verandah, arranged so that there is a continuous vista terminating in water and boats. The layout of this project departs from the usual scheme by breaking up the interior into a number of separate pavilions. A similar approach is followed by Alexander Tzannes in his masonry villa in Bellevue Hill, which juxtaposes two masonry wings, each topped with a typical suburban gable. The interior is comfortably finished, with warmly toned colours and fabrics.

The house by Engelen Moore at Neutral Bay returns to the well-established suburban layout of a sequence of rooms opening off a side corridor, a sensible solution for a narrow site. The interior is illuminated by a side wall of louvred glass, together with a quartet of sawtooth lights set into the roof. Additional light is provided by a glazed court covered with an awning. The minimalist interior is rigorous, with white-only walls, furniture and built-in cupboards, complemented by white ceramic fittings for kitchen and bathroom. Another late

Ed Lippman's house in Mosman, Sydney

Nonda Katsalidis's apartments in St Kilda, Melbourne

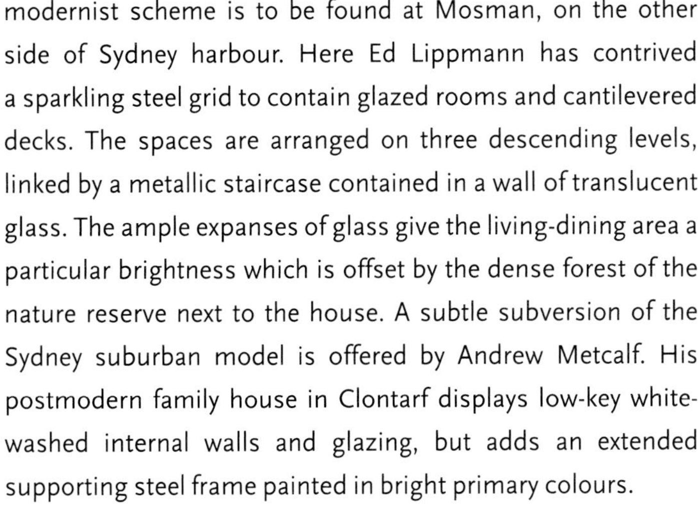

modernist scheme is to be found at Mosman, on the other side of Sydney harbour. Here Ed Lippmann has contrived a sparkling steel grid to contain glazed rooms and cantilevered decks. The spaces are arranged on three descending levels, linked by a metallic staircase contained in a wall of translucent glass. The ample expanses of glass give the living-dining area a particular brightness which is offset by the dense forest of the nature reserve next to the house. A subtle subversion of the Sydney suburban model is offered by Andrew Metcalf. His postmodern family house in Clontarf displays low-key white-washed internal walls and glazing, but adds an extended supporting steel frame painted in bright primary colours.

Among the late modernist suburban houses dotted around other parts of the country is Ross Chisholm's suavely modelled balcony house in Mosman Park, a suburb of Perth. Translucent glass surfaces are a special feature of this project, as may be seen in the entrance court of the house and the sliding screens separating the living and dining areas. Elsewhere, there is a preference for warmly toned textures rather than the unvarying whiteness of the Sydney designers. The pavilion extension by Carr Design for a traditional Toorak home in Melbourne also focuses on a glazed interior space. Metallic louvres in the side wall can be raised to reveal the adjacent tennis court and garden beyond. A more extravagant version of this glasshouse idea is seen in an extension to a Victorian family mansion in nearby Kew. The transparent shed-like wing of this project, designed by Glenn Murcutt in association with the firm of Bates Smart, functions as an independent dwelling, complete with living, dining, cooking and sleeping areas, not to mention an indoor pool. No expense has been spared in this project which exploits tinted glass for the mechanically operated windows and roof hood.

The Melbourne architect Sean Godsell returns to more conventional mid-century modernist principles for his own residence in the same suburb. But the glass panels that encase his tightly planned, rectangular house on four sides are clad in an unusual rusting steel grille. The tactile roughness of this feature is highlighted by the dramatic device of cantilevering the body of the building outwards from a sloping earthen bank. Protruding into the suburban street, the house seems to challenge its neighbours, but in fact conforms with them by its insistence on a discreet and comfortable interior. In the end, suburban privacy triumphs over architectural exhibitionism!

BALCONY HOUSE, MOSMAN PARK, PERTH

translucent textures

Completed by the architect Ross Chisholm shortly before his death in 1998, this house rises in a pyramid of balconied masses above a street in a fashionable riverside suburb of Perth. The design employs a variety of glass surfaces, either as transparent panes or as polished blocks, to achieve a translucent quality that pervades the entrance court as well as the interior living, dining and sleeping spaces. All of these occupy the upper level of the house; the lower level is reserved for guest accommodation.

top left The balconies of the house as seen from the street

left The conservatory between the master bedroom and the garden

above White leather furniture in the living-dining area

opposite above Glass bricks and louvred glazing help to filter the light

opposite below A pivoting glass door leads into the partly glazed entrance court

domestic industrial flair

Overlooking Sydney's Middle Harbour from the gentle hills of suburban Clontarf, Andrew Metcalf's house is a sparkling essay in domestic industrial style. Factory-like steelwork and glass bricks are adapted with considerable flair to the requirements and scale of family living. Like many Sydney dwellings, the house is built on a sloping site, with the entrance at the upper level leading directly to the living and dining areas. The kitchen is located at the top of a spiral staircase which descends to the bedrooms at the lower level. These open directly onto a deck with the obligatory swimming pool. Throughout, the strengths of the industrial style – with its bold and imaginative use of glass and metal – make an aesthetically comfortable setting for domestic needs, much enhanced by glorious harbour views.

above Brightly toned steel girders encase the curving glass wall at the rear of the house

right Translucent glass bricks and clear glass windows light the dining area

opposite Yellow furniture in the living area complements the painted steelwork

TRIPLE-WING HOUSE, TOORAK, MELBOURNE

glass walls and floating ceiling

opposite above The walk-through closet attached to the upstairs master bedroom

opposite below The kitchen in the middle of the pavilion wing is a small enclosure lined with wooden surfaces that opens onto the breakfast area

left The corridor leading from the breakfast area to the children's wing

below The family dining area at one end of the pavilion wing

Designed by Andrew Norbury for his own family, this residence in Melbourne's leafy Toorak is conceived as three discrete wings, partly separated by planted garden courts. The double-storey entrance wing closest to the street houses a glazed living room as well as the staircase. This ascends to the master bedroom, from which a walk-through dressing closet leads to the bathroom. The intermediate wing is a lofty rectangular pavilion with a curved plywood ceiling that appears to float above glass walls. In it are located the kitchen, the breakfast area and the family dining space. The third wing, which extends towards the rear of the site, is the domain of three boys, and contains bedrooms, bathrooms and a play area.

HOUSE WITH SAWTOOTH LIGHTS, NEUTRAL BAY, SYDNEY

rethinking the suburban model

Designed by the architects Engelen Moore, this narrow house is an inspired late modernist interpretation of a standard suburban layout. At street level, the house consists of three bedrooms and a single bathroom opening off a black-walled corridor on one side, with full-height windows shaded by aluminium louvres on the other. Further lighting is provided by sawtooth roof lights. As the land dips towards the rear, the side corridor becomes a flight of steps descending to a double-height living space. The kitchen-dining area is sited beneath a glazed court.

opposite above Only the blank walls and sawtooth lights of the house are visible from the street, the entrance being concealed in the blackened recess to the left

opposite below The double-height living space at the rear of the house, showing the kitchen-dining area at the end

left The master bedroom opens onto the glazed court which is provided with a motorized awning

below The side corridor beside the master bedroom with stairs down to the living space

ARCHITECT'S RESIDENCE, KEW, MELBOURNE

uncompromising simplicity

The architect Sean Godsell chose an uncompromising layout for this simplest of houses intended for his own family. The living-dining-cooking space takes up almost three-quarters of the rectangular interior, with three bedrooms and a small bathroom tucked into one side. Wall-to-ceiling glass panels encase the house on three sides, opening it up to the suburban Melbourne street into which it protrudes. Privacy and protection are ensured by a rusting steel grille that runs almost continuously around the outside.

opposite above An electrically operated grille folds out to serve as an entrance canopy

opposite below The furniture at one end of the living space clusters around the fireplace recessed into the wall

above left and right The house as seen from the street, cantilevered out over the front garden. The rusted patination of the steel grille provides constantly changing patterns and colours, depending on the light

below The other end of the interior is dominated by a dining/work table

'sculpture with plumbing'

The architect Tom Kovac is responsible for the quip at the head of this page which reveals the sculptural imagination that underlies his remarkable project. Commissioned by a doctor and his wife, the house fits easily into Melbourne's grassy suburbs, its curving whitewashed walls snaking in and out of the trees. The curving walls continue inside, dividing the interior into two discrete zones, one housing a small surgery, kitchen and pantry, the other a pair of sharply pointed bedrooms. The void in between is given over to a living-dining space, with a glass wall at the rear.

opposite The central living space is roofed with an undulating ceiling that echoes the overall layout of the house

left An indoor swimming pool, running from the living area to the outdoor court, follows the sinuous line of the exterior wall

above and below Even the island bench in the middle of the kitchen is composed of curves

ATRIUM HOUSE, COORPAROO, BRISBANE

intricate timberwork

above A shaft of stainless steel is suspended over the cooking range in the kitchen

right Shuttered and louvred wooden windows encase a corner seating area in the master bedroom

This elaborate villa is a grandiose addition to an otherwise modest Brisbane suburb. Conceived by the architects Donovan Hill as a sequence of ascending and interlocking spaces, many intended for formal living, the villa exploits the rich textural possibilities of intricately worked timber set into a finely finished concrete frame. The core of the house is an atrium-like space that functions as both a lobby and an outdoor living area. Steps and corridors from here lead to the more private parts of the house.

above The street façade is an assemblage of projecting balconies overlooking a formal garden and a swimming pool

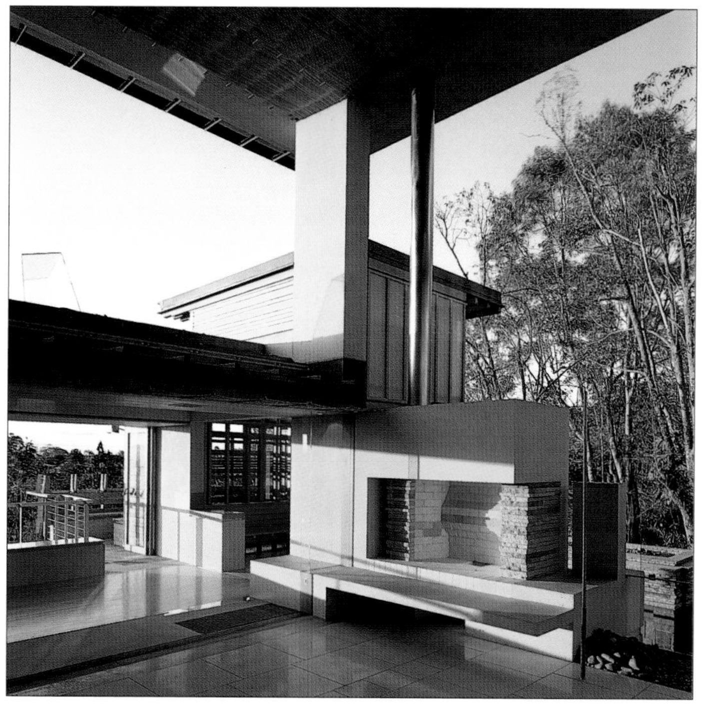

right The lobby is roofed over but not fully enclosed, to create an open room complete with outdoor cooking facilities

PAVILION EXTENSION, TOORAK, MELBOURNE

renovating and reinventing

above The house with its glazed pavilion extension as seen from the tennis court

below The renovated dining room in the original house

In their refurbishment of an early twentieth-century mansion in Melbourne's elegant Toorak, Carr Design took the opportunity of adding a contrasting, glazed pavilion to accommodate a new living area and study. This wing is connected to the original house by means of a glazed lobby. The new living area, furnished exclusively in tones of white and grey, has a polished bluestone floor and a gently curved, perforated ceiling. The fireplace is detached from the full-height windows of the end wall, while the side wall, entirely of glass, looks out over the tennis court.

above The original kitchen-dining area with polished wooden floor and stainless steel fittings

left The U-shaped galley kitchen has a red rubber floor and a suspended stainless steel vent

right The study opening off the living area

opposite The glazed lobby with Akio Makigawa's marble and granite sculptures

below Interior of the new living area showing the end fireplace and side wall of glass with electrically operated louvres

waterside living

Tucked into a narrow, steeply sloping site leading down to the water, this house by Alex Popov is divided into three detached pavilions distributed on two levels. The kitchen-dining and living-sleeping areas are accommodated in two separate pavilions on the lower level. A small court in between these has a sunken pool and a side wall lined with blue tiles. Glass doors fold back to create an uninterrupted space marked by a limestone floor running the full length of the building. A third pavilion on the upper level has a studio beneath and a timber-slatted garage above leading to the street.

opposite The dining room is positioned between the interior court and the harbourside quay

far left The house seen fom the water

left The studio-garage wing above and living wing beneath separated by a court

below The bedroom over the living area

textural surprises

Dale Jones-Evans takes delight in this suburban house in Melbourne, punctuating it with protruding weatherboard cubes and adding zinc tiles to the upper walls. The result is a richly textured and strongly volumetric house that embodies all that is best in postmodernism. The layout is unconventional, with clearly articulated living, dining and kitchen areas grouped around three sides of a rectangular pool. The kitchen extends outwards with windows on three sides. A flying gallery at the upper level provides access to the three bedrooms, one of which projects out over the pool.

above Thick planting in front of the zinc cladding of one of the upper bedrooms

right Stairs from the living area at the front of the house lead up to the gallery

left The side of the house showing the weatherboard-clad upper bedroom projecting out over the blue-tiled pool

above The kitchen has long windows on two sides and small windows set into the end wall

above The flying gallery connecting the upper bedrooms

PLYWOOD HOUSE, ST LUCIA, BRISBANE

verandah living

For his own residence set on a sloping site in one of Brisbane's verdant suburbs, the architect Bud Brannigan turned to the traditional Queenslander for inspiration. Elevated well above the ground, the house is clad in plywood and fibro panels and protected from the rain by generous overhangs of corrugated metal. Family activities are focused on an extended outdoor living space set between the kitchen in the middle of the house and an enclosed living room in front. Bedrooms are positioned at the back and at the upper level.

opposite above The house from the street, with the garage below and the living room above, its window shaded by a freely hanging wooden blind

opposite below A continuous verandah runs along the side of the house, looking over the garden

below An outdoor living space on the extended verandah, with the kitchen to one side

a challenge to the suburbs

Geoff Lovie's polychromed timber-clad house strikes a subversive note in the conservative suburbs of Canberra's twin city. Not content with painting the entire building in a violent purple, Lovie adds angled wooden window frames, free-form balcony panels and out-of-kilter overhangs, all in bright yellow. Such formalistic and colouristic touches give the exterior a cheeky, light-hearted character which contrasts with the natural timbers and white surfaces of the interior. Like so many other new houses, Lovie's project demonstrates that Australians often focus their creative interests on the outside rather than the inside of their dwellings.

above left The free-form, cut-out balcony panel overlooking the street contrasts effectively with the box-like proportions of the house

above right The rising land on which the house is built is overlooked by angled wooden window frames

top a wooden bridge links the rear garden to the upper level

opposite Cooking and dining on the upper level are separated from the living zone by the staircase well

mediterranean mode

Alexander Tzannes designed this spacious residential project in a Mediterranean mode, with warmly toned, solid masonry surfaces. The well-articulated gables of the house, however, are perfectly in keeping with the suburban vernacular of this elegant Sydney suburb. The principal wing accommodates the garage, the servants' quarters, the formal living and dining areas, and the master bedroom, all on successive levels. A secondary wing contains the kitchen-family room, with the children's bedrooms above.

opposite above The two wings of the house rising above the swimming pool

opposite below A comfortably furnished living area adjoins the kitchen

left A balcony with a harbour view opens off the master bedroom at the upper level

below The formal living room at the front of the house has pastel-toned furniture grouped around an unusually tall fireplace

FAMILY VILLA, CAULFIELD, MELBOURNE

monumental formality

This imposing villa in Melbourne's Caulfield, designed by Wood Marsh, is intended for formal reception, as is obvious from the impressive proportions of the interior spaces. The house is laid out in three discrete sections: an ellipse of concrete containing the lobby and study, a rectangular, glazed living-dining area with bedrooms above, and an angled wing accommodating the kitchen and laundry. The textures of terrazzo, stone and concrete are offset by stainless steel and mirrored glass to produce a sombre, monumental effect.

opposite above A metal-clad 'portcullis', containing the master bathroom, protrudes outwards from the elliptical concrete lobby

opposite below A stainless steel and glass display unit separates the living and dining spaces

left and top The elliptical lobby with circular skylight is dominated by a sweeping staircase lined with a steel-panelled balustrade; this ascends to the master bedroom

above A projection of the skylight moves up the staircase with the passage of time

ANGLED WING HOUSE, RUSHCUTTERS BAY, SYDNEY

vertical progressions

Designed by Neil Durbach and Camilla Block for an artist and his family, this house is divided into two angled wings to fit into a tiny sloping site with an old stone retaining wall running up the middle. The left-hand wing accommodates the principal living-dining space, at the rear of which is a kitchen with a study above. The right-hand wing comprises two levels of bedrooms and bathrooms. Steps ascend from the middle of the house to a rooftop deck with a small swimming pool beyond.

left A small garden court opens up at the back of the timber-lined kitchen

above The two wings of the house angle outwards to take advantage of the harbour view

opposite The timber-floored double-storey living and dining area is overlooked by a narrow gallery

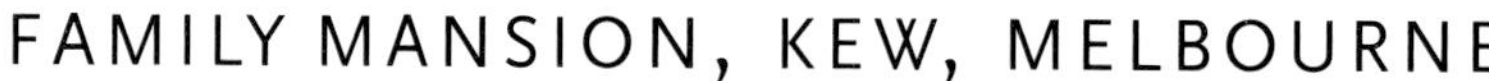

FAMILY MANSION, KEW, MELBOURNE

glasshouse living

After purchasing an historic Italianate mansion in Kew, this family commissioned Glenn Murcutt in association with Robert Bruce of Bates Smart to design an additional two-storey, Victorian-inspired glasshouse for them. The long structure has windows on both sides, looking out over the garden to the front, and is connected by a court to the original house to the rear. The luxuriously appointed interior incorporates a double-height living area, a dining space for twenty guests, and a covered swimming pool.

opposite above The garden façade is overhung by laminated glass hoods that pivot upwards

left The double-height living space in the middle of the house is lit by clear glass panels; the upper panels pivot upwards

above The original mansion with the glasshouse extension

below The extension from the garden showing the curved lead roof ending in a continuous laminated glass sun hood

top left The kitchen-dining area at one end of the house, with essential services concealed in the white-painted block to the side

opposite centre Access to services behind the kitchen area is concealed beneath the staircase

opposite below One of the upstairs bedrooms tucked into the roof

above The double-height space makes an ideal environment for formal entertainment, with its long, polished dining table for a large number of guests

complex geometries

The variable curves of Ivan Rijavec's house in Templestowe, one of Melbourne's sprawling eastern developments, provide welcome relief from the quadrangular suburban surroundings. Almost devoid of right angles, the house sweeps outwards in a number of prow-shaped projections that contain the living-dining area, the principal bedroom and a barbecue deck. The complex geometry of the façade and interior spaces is emphasized by bright colours that add to the overall patterning effect, thereby defying the monotony of the surrounding houses.

above The house's exterior presents a continuous sequence of angled and curved surfaces, animated by conspicuous coloured bands

right The rear entrance of the house is sheltered by a boat-like wooden canopy

left At the top of the staircase a curving wall of shelves contains the island kitchen

opposite The island kitchen in the middle of the upper living-dining area

Miele

Bathing boxes at Brighton in Melbourne

19
20

BEACH

All of the major Australian cities are situated on or near the ocean. Sydney, for instance, is built around an indented harbour ideal for boating, with its eastern suburbs facing directly onto magnificent sandy beaches. For Sydneysiders as well as those who live in other cities, swimming, surfing and sailing are possible on an almost daily basis in the summer months. Generations of suburban Australians have lived near the water, creating an authentic beach culture which is still very much alive. Spurning the nearest seaside location in their quest for the ideal beach, Australians do not hesitate to abandon the cities at holiday times for more distant resorts, especially those offering the best surfing. For holidaymakers with a bigger budget, there are the luxury island locations of the Barrier Reef. These conform to the popular stereotype of the tropical paradise resort, equipped with swaying palm trees, white sand and turquoise waters.

The earliest incarnation of the beach house in Australia was probably a simple wooden hut for changing, and for storing towels and umbrellas. Early twentieth-century boxes at Brighton in Melbourne are now freshly painted in response to a growing appreciation of these primitive precursors of beach culture. A later development was the fibro-cement shack which sprang up at weekend locales outside all the coastal cities and towns from the mid-century onwards. Though these unpretentious timber-framed structures, invariably clad in inexpensive fibro panels, were of little distinction, they provided uncluttered living areas and decks looking out over the ocean. Many such shacks are now being resuscitated in a bid to recapture the innocence of an earlier, simpler age.

Some new beach houses are consciously designed to emulate the original fibro shack, seeking new expressions for

Bondi Beach, Sydney

this simplest of all recreational structures. Peter Maddison's towered cabin on Phillip Island, two hours from Melbourne, is little more than one room on top of another, furnished in the most elementary manner. Outside, the house is articulated by angled timber trusses, slatted decking and louvred sun guards. A more extended structural scheme using timber framing and fibro-cement panels is the curved-canopy marina residence of John Mainwaring at Noosa Waters on Queensland's Sunshine Coast. Rejecting the angled roof that inevitably crowns the archetypal beach shack, the architect has created a lightweight curving canopy that gives the upper level of the house an unexpected flowing profile. The interior living-dining area with its efficient workbenches recalls the prototype which it surpasses through the use of finely worked and brightly painted surfaces.

Designers of beach houses often display a preference for timber cladding, seeking a weathered wooden look that recalls the beach shacks and boathouses of the past. Nick Tridente's wooden-frame house in North Haven's marina, for example, only a short distance from Adelaide's busy centre, has a boldly articulated façade with fully expressed wooden posts framing recessed plywood panels. A nautical atmosphere pervades the interior which has wooden floors, kitchen bench and wall cupboards, all smoothly finished. John Wardle's beach house at Balnarring on the Mornington Peninsula, an hour south of Melbourne, is almost entirely clad in timber. Cedar plywood faded from exposure to the sea air contrasts with better-preserved, polished timber battens, creating a visually appealing variety of textures. Glazing is restricted on the sides, giving the house the appearance of an oceanside shelter that fits comfortably into the surrounding scrubland.

Nonda Katsalidis's oceanside bunker at nearby St Andrews Beach is another exercise in contrasting materials. Cast iron girders frame the glazed living-kitchen room, while wooden supports and panels encase the adjacent sleeping zone.

Bedarra Island in the Whitsunday Passage, Queensland

On the shores of the Indian Ocean near Broome, Western Australia

Port Sorell on the north coast of Tasmania

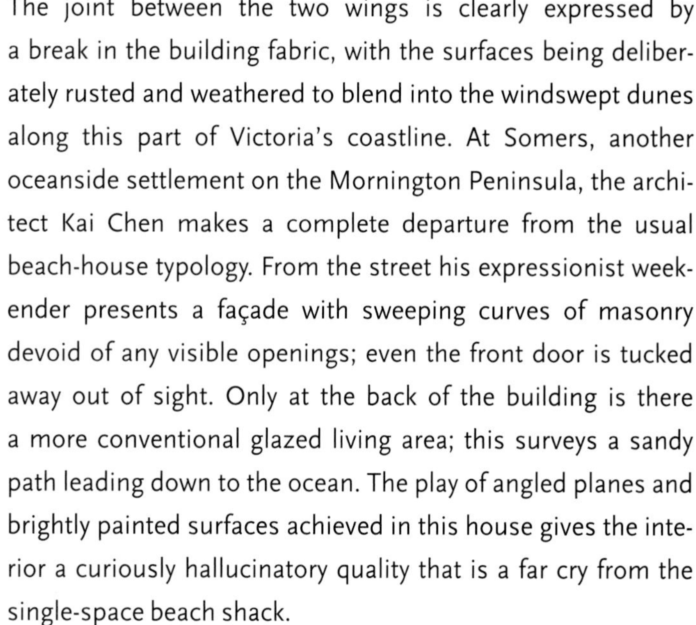

The joint between the two wings is clearly expressed by a break in the building fabric, with the surfaces being deliberately rusted and weathered to blend into the windswept dunes along this part of Victoria's coastline. At Somers, another oceanside settlement on the Mornington Peninsula, the architect Kai Chen makes a complete departure from the usual beach-house typology. From the street his expressionist weekender presents a façade with sweeping curves of masonry devoid of any visible openings; even the front door is tucked away out of sight. Only at the back of the building is there a more conventional glazed living area; this surveys a sandy path leading down to the ocean. The play of angled planes and brightly painted surfaces achieved in this house gives the interior a curiously hallucinatory quality that is a far cry from the single-space beach shack.

With its much warmer climate, Queensland offers opportunities for lightweight construction. Beach houses in and around Brisbane and Noosa often achieve a high degree of transparency, with interiors transformed into deck-like spaces. The open-webbed weekend house belonging to the architects Brit Andresen and Peter O'Gorman on Stradbroke Island, easily accessible from Brisbane, is a delicately textured building that makes little distinction between inside and outside. The dining area is surrounded by wooden slats with gaps in between offering tantalizing glimpses of the nearby ocean. This space is separated from the living zone by a sandy open court which makes use of the same slats, thereby visually dissolving the difference between inside and outside. The bedrooms above employ plywood flaps that can be angled outwards to capture the sea breeze. Gerard Murtagh's eccentric slatted weekender on a sloping dune above Sunshine Beach consciously sets out to avoid the glare and saltiness of the environment. A bunker, the house has a main balcony which becomes an enclosed deck opening off the kitchen-dining area. Only by opening the louvred shutters is it possible to enjoy the view. The weathered plywood slats of the exterior are suspended above the sand, giving the house a floating, boat-like quality.

This boarded type of beach house is not necessarily restricted to the hotter climates of Australia, something borne out by Edmond and Corrigan's weatherboard house at Seaton Cove on Tasmania's rugged northeast shore. The outstanding

A Bondi Beach life-saving class

Surfers Paradise, Queensland

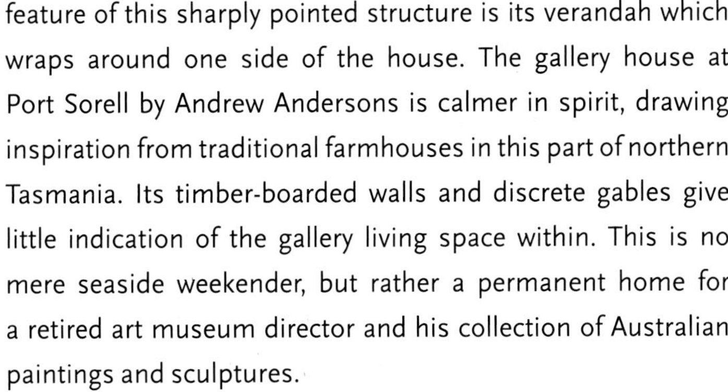

feature of this sharply pointed structure is its verandah which wraps around one side of the house. The gallery house at Port Sorell by Andrew Andersons is calmer in spirit, drawing inspiration from traditional farmhouses in this part of northern Tasmania. Its timber-boarded walls and discrete gables give little indication of the gallery living space within. This is no mere seaside weekender, but rather a permanent home for a retired art museum director and his collection of Australian paintings and sculptures.

Parallel to the trend for timbered beach houses such as these is a preference for more expensively built and luxuriously appointed projects. That Australians are now retiring to ocean-side locations is evident in the number of well-appointed and spaciously laid-out villas and houses that are intended as permanent residences. Polished wooden decks and verandahs extending outwards from glazed living areas are obligatory features of such houses; so too are whitewashed masonry walls and large windows set in metallic frames. The majority of these projects, seen in ever-increasing numbers clinging to the cliffs and spreading over the dunes that line Australia's eastern shore, suffer from anonymity; a few outstanding examples demonstrate that architectural ingenuity may still be found beside the ocean.

One of the most extraordinary of Australia's solidly built beach houses is Barrie Marshall's subterranean retreat on Phillip Island. Dug deep into the dunes, the walls and roof of this house are concealed beneath sloping sandbanks. Visitors enter through a sunken grassy court, protected from the glare and wind on four sides by concrete ramparts which accommodate garage, stores and services. Once inside the house they are confronted with a dazzling seascape that pervades the interior through an almost continuous wall of glass. An equally spectacular panorama is enjoyed by the inhabitants of Renato D'Ettore's extravagant palazzo on the sandstone cliffs at Coogee, overlooking the Pacific. This impressive project is intended for formal living, with a suite of symmetrically disposed reception dining areas linked by a corridor built up against the cliff at the rear. All the rooms enjoy ocean outlooks, and there is even a specially designed belvedere on the upper level reached by a suspended walkway. Here, as in so many other beach houses, the view entirely dominates the interior, testifying to the irresistible lure of sea and sky.

oceanside grandeur

Renato D'Ettore's majestic project in Sydney's Coogee was designed for his relations. The house is arranged on two levels, with corridors next to the cliff at the rear of the site reached by a protruding square staircase tower. The lower level is given over to a linked sequence of formal seating areas, with a sunken fireplace zone at one end and the dining area at the other; the upper level has bedrooms at the ends and in the centre a curving belvedere reached by a bridge. The rooms are laid out according to a strict geometry that creates axial vistas of the ocean from all parts of the house.

above The seating area in the middle of the living space offers a matchless panorama of the ocean

right Only a glass barrier separates the swimming pool in front of the house from the ocean below

left The house perched on cliffs overlooking the Pacific

right The bridge leading from the corridor of the house to the belvedere with wood-lined square openings in the walls and glass-brick skylights in the ceiling

opposite above The family TV room is hidden from the formal areas beyond

opposite below The master bedroom on the upper level filled with dawn light

above The curving shower-bath with mosaic tiling, part of the master bedroom suite

left A glimpse of the kitchen from the corridor

opposite The corridor at the rear of the house is lined by slit windows, with the staircase flanked by balustrades finished in blue stucco

GALLERY HOUSE, PORT SORELL, TASMANIA

traditional tasmanian

Commissioned by a retired art-museum director, the architect Andrew Andersons decided on a traditional design for this house on Tasmania's untamed northern coast. Two bedrooms with generous bay windows linked by a glazed corridor look out over the waters of Bass Strait. A long living-dining room with a recessed stove at one end serves as the core of the house. The skylight running the full length of the gabled ceiling illuminates the numerous works of art.

left The house stands in a forest of tea trees and oaks that sweeps down to the ocean

below The central room of the house, designed for the display of works of art, also functions as a comfortable living space focused on a fireplace set into the end wall

opposite above The gabled wing of one of the bedrooms with its projecting bay window

opposite below Glowing perspex boxes rescued from a gallery installation illuminate a geometric wall sculpture in wood

GALLERY HOUSE, PORT SORELL, TASMANIA

left A pair of grey metal G'DAY chairs (whose structure spells out the classic Australian greeting), designed by Brian Sayer and Christopher Connell

below The glazed and tiled corridor provides a transition from the central living-dining room to the outdoor balcony on which a pair of G'DAY chairs have been placed

opposite above A seating area at the end of the balcony

opposite below The guest bedroom with its comfortable chair and projecting bay window

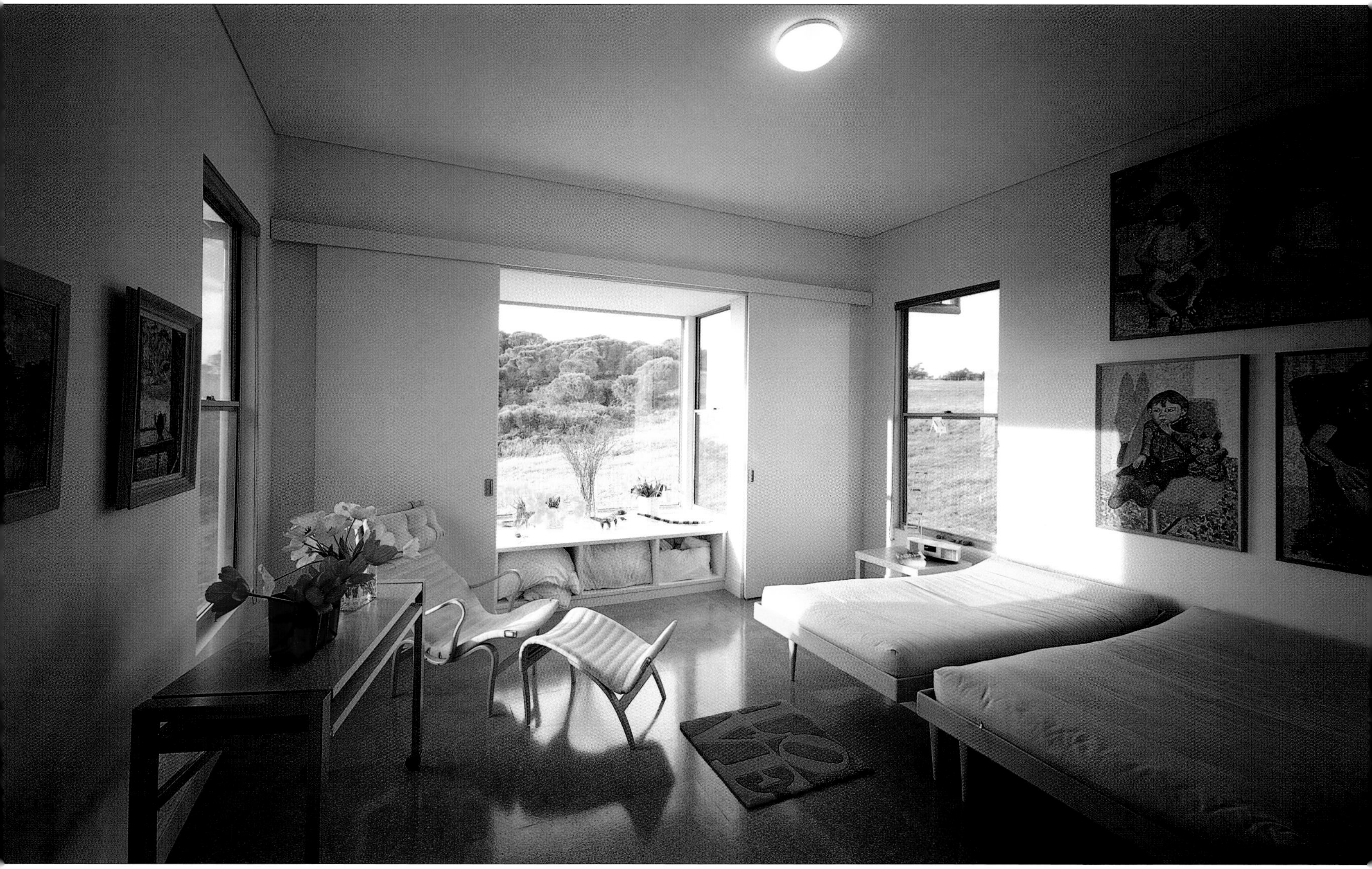

filtering the ocean glare

For their weekends beside the ocean at this popular island resort near Brisbane, the architects Brit Andresen and Peter O'Gorman have fashioned an airy, open-webbed house that offers views at every opportunity. A sandy court forms its core, separating the kitchen-dining area from the living space, both of double height. A mezzanine gallery running along one side gives access to simple sleeping boxes, terminating in a belvedere at the front which is used for outdoor dining. The resultant effect is one of exhilarating transparency, dissolving the boundaries between inside and outside.

opposite Looking across the sandy court towards the interior dining area, with the balustraded gallery on one side

far left View of the house from the garden showing the steps leading up to the raised gallery

left A side corridor runs along the two-metre wide spine of the house

below The slatted frame over the court

OCEANSIDE BUNKER, ST ANDREWS BEACH, VICTORIA

weathered textures

above The house is surrounded by the windswept brush that lines the sandy shore of Victoria's Mornington Peninsula

right A break in the building fabric marks the transition between the living-dining area and the sleeping wing

opposite above The living-dining area at one end of the house has walls of glass, through which the ocean may clearly be seen, topped with rusting metal panels

The rusting and weathered textures of this house, used by the architect Nonda Katsalidis and his family for seaside escapes from Melbourne, are perfectly in keeping with Victoria's ocean wilderness. So too is the bunker-like massing of the house, laid out in a single rectangular wing with clearly separated living-dining and sleeping areas. This functional division is accentuated by contrasts in the metallic and wooden materials of which the house is built.

above At the end of the living-dining part of the house, a slit window rises between recycled timber planks

above At the other end of the house, the sleeping area, thick recycled timber insulates and gives privacy to the bedrooms. The formal composition remains harmonious within the rugged natural landscape

TOWERED CABIN, PHILLIP ISLAND, VICTORIA

oceanside lookout

In this smallest of beach huts the architect Peter Maddison links two superimposed rooms with a spiral staircase that ascends to the rooftop. The lower level houses bedroom and bathroom, while the upper has a kitchen-living area opening onto a timber deck. The deck is supported on struts and is shielded by an angled and louvred overhang. The contrast between these strongly expressed timber components and the flat fibro wall cladding, together with the project's diminutive scale, gives the house an almost Japanese appearance.

left The timber deck, carried on triangular struts, gives the house the appearance of a lifeguard's lookout tower

opposite An essential part of any beach house in chilly Victoria, the fireplace is incorporated into the kitchen

below Looking down on the living-dining area; glass doors lead out onto the deck

WOODEN-FRAME HOUSE, NORTH HAVEN, ADELAIDE

boathouse dreams

Built for a yacht enthusiast working in Adelaide, Nick Tridente's boldly articulated wooden-frame house at North Haven marina sits comfortably among the masts and sails. The project is conceived in the manner of a boathouse, with little attempt to conceal the firmly bolted posts, beams and joists. The fabric of the building is recessed into this structural grid, giving the exterior a jaunty, makeshift appearance. This impression is belied by the interior, whose sleekly finished wooden surfaces and joinery are a perfect setting for fine furniture and works of art.

left A comfortable corner from which to enjoy the waterside view

below The tightly planned kitchen, with its efficiently designed island bench, gives the interior a distinctly nautical character

opposite above The house overlooks the marina

opposite below Gleaming wooden floors and columns frame the spacious living zone, with sliding windows leading onto the deck

SLATTED WEEKENDER, SUNSHINE BEACH, QUEENSLAND

sheltered from sun and wind

Gerard Murtagh's holiday house for city professionals on Queensland's Sunshine Beach shuns all exposure to the ocean to present a windowless façade. The application of weathered plywood all over the house gives it a slatted bunker-like look. At the lower level the house comprises a kitchen-dining area opening onto an extended deck entirely encased in slatted timbers. Only by opening the shuttered flaps can the ocean be viewed. At the upper level there is a pair of children's bedrooms and a living area with access to a rooftop deck.

left A slatted lower deck opens off the living-dining area

above The slatted exterior of the house with shuttered flaps opening off the lower deck

opposite Full-height glass doors fold back leading from the kitchen-dining area to the enclosed deck

above The rooftop deck shielded from light and wind by timber baffles

designed for cyclones

The result of a unique collaboration between the architect Glenn Murcutt and a renowned female aboriginal artist, this pavilion studio stands near freshwater mangroves within sight of the Arafura Sea in coastal Arnhem Land. Raised up on stilts well above the ground, the house has been built to withstand the cyclones that threaten this part of the Northern Territory. A secure metal frame is roofed with a gable of corrugated iron topped with vents. Plywood shutters open up to allow strong winds to pass through the building without damaging its structure.

above The north side of the house is lined with red-brown plywood shutters that angle outwards, ventilating five sleeping bays and the living-cooking area at the end

right Cool breezes through the shutter system make it pleasant for family and guests to share the television in the large open living space

below Aboriginal children on the steps of the house

opposite The simply appointed living-cooking area is dominated by metal roof trusses

SUBTERRANEAN RETREAT, PHILLIP ISLAND, VICTORIA

resisting the elements

Dug deep down into the dunes overlooking a faraway beach, Barrie Marshall's house on Phillip Island is designed to withstand the bracing climate of Victoria's harsh ocean shore. The residential wing is approached through a square court protected by concrete ramparts containing garage and stores. Beyond lies the house itself. Windows on its far side offer panoramic oceanscapes from the central kitchen-dining area and the end living rooms. A corridor leads to a suite of three bedrooms, interspersed with bathrooms, all with views. The untreated concrete wall surfaces, polished blackened floor and stainless steel room-dividers give the interior a gleaming quality that reflects the ocean dazzle.

top A concrete-lined gap in the dunes is the only indication of the house from outside

left and above The polished concrete pavement of the corridor reflects the floor-level windows

left The steel-flanked entrance to the main wing from the enclosed grassy court

top right A view of the ocean from behind the kitchen-dining area

centre right The living area at the end of the house with its fireplace set into the wall

bottom right Concrete, steel and leather are the only materials in this austere bedroom

WEATHERBOARD HOUSE, SEATON COVE, TASMANIA

beach moderne

Intended for two doctors and their grown-up family, this triple-storeyed house overlooks an isolated beach on Tasmania's northwest coast. To exploit the magnificent views, the architects Edmond and Corrigan have provided a living-dining-kitchen area with an elliptical end window that looks out over the rocks and ocean. The dull-green and pale-blue tones of the weatherboard cladding help to integrate the house into its wooded site.

top The house on its sloping site showing the elliptical window at its narrow end

above A weather vane marks the summit of the roof

opposite The dining table echoes the elliptical void in the wall beyond

above The open verandah with continuous seating wraps around one side of the living-dining area

below Views of the ocean may be enjoyed from the raised bed

weathered, varnished and polished

Intended for a narrow site surrounded by scrubby bush on the ocean's edge on Victoria's Mornington Peninsula, John Wardle's long, thin beach house is almost entirely clad in plywood. The cedar fabric is cut out to create decks, slatted window shields, and frames for recessed glass panels, giving the house a strongly volumetric quality. Textural variety is achieved through weathered panels, varnished battens and polished interior timberwork. The house features an unusual cantilevered living space that steps up from the central kitchen-dining area so as to look out through the trees to the ocean.

opposite The dramatically cantilevered end of the house accommodates the living space

left Side view, showing the entrance deck placed between the living and sleeping zones

below A wood stove and full-height storage boxes, together with a change of level, demarcate the living and dining areas

left The dining room, filled with glowing sunlight, containing a custom-built plywood table

right The corridor-study between the kitchen and master bedroom has floor-level windows

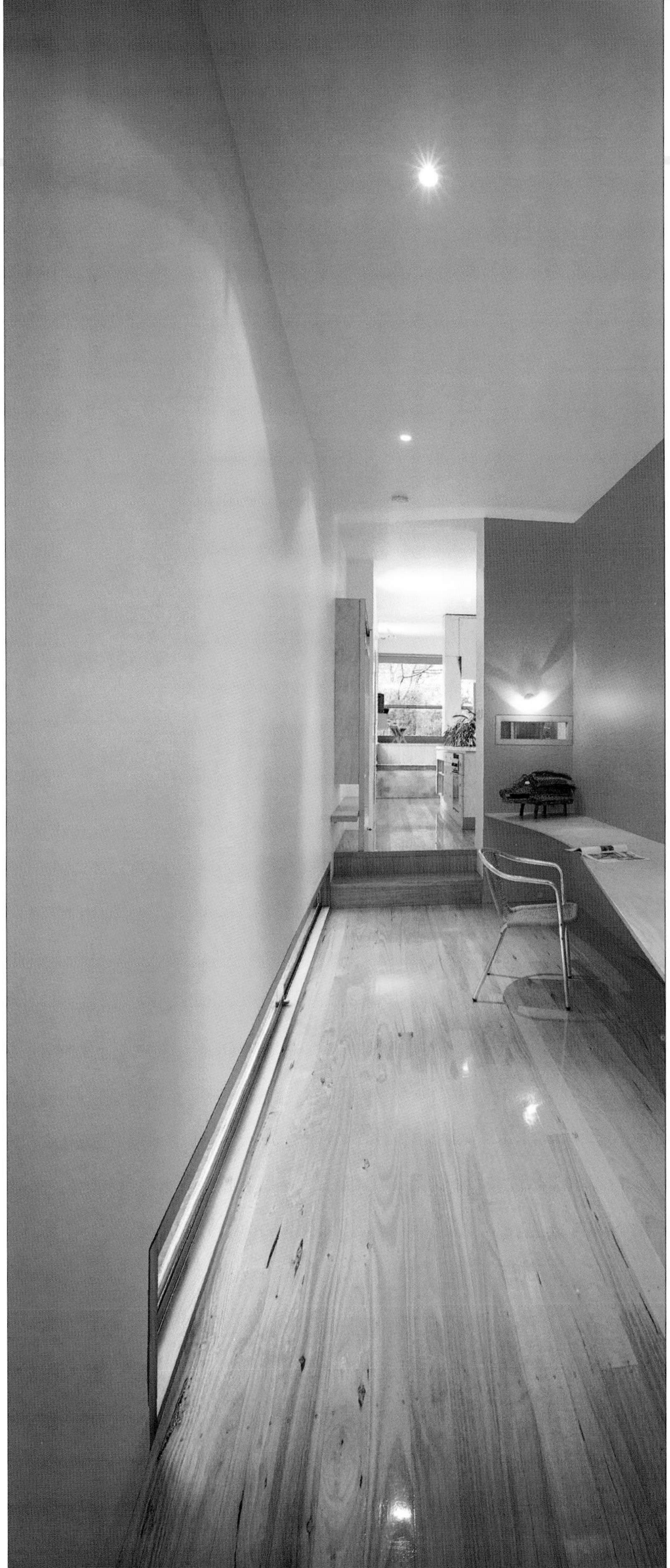

floating iron

Located in the vicinity of the beach resort of Noosa on Queensland's Sunshine Coast, John Mainwaring's family home is built of traditional plywood and fibro panels but topped with an unusual curving canopy of corrugated iron. This gives the house a striking lightweight, almost floating, quality. The lower level is conceived as an open living space, leading to the children's bedrooms and play area. The main bedroom and adjoining studio are located on the upper level.

above The house at night as reflected in the waters of the marina

opposite The curving roof lined with plywood dominates the main bedroom. Small windows shaded by metal louvres set near to the floor offer views of the water from the bed itself. The gallery to the right looks down onto the living area

above The living area, the core of the house, makes ample use of timbered textures with stainless steel for the kitchen beyond

left The house, dominated by its curving canopy of corrugated iron

below Narrow slatted windows light the bathroom adjoining the main bedroom

colours, curves and angles

With its display of curving surfaces, slanting walls and brightly toned panels, Kai Chen's expressionist beach house is easily distinguished from its shack-like neighbours on Victoria's Mornington Peninsula. The exterior is an exercise in striking contrasts: to the street, the house presents a sweep of darkly toned and curving stuccoed masonry that almost engulfs the entrance door; to the rear, a wall of glass opens up to the sandy path that leads down to the beach.

opposite left above Sweeping curves of masonry lead from the street to the concealed entrance

opposite left below The rectilinear glazed living-dining area abuts the curving masonry bulk containing the principal bedroom

opposite right Brightly painted sloping walls lit by narrow window strips line the corridor leading to the bedrooms

above The pale tones of the living-dining area are illuminated by an angled skylight. The front wall of glass looks over the dunes

above A ladder climbs to the mezzanine over the main bedroom

right Looking down on the main bedroom from the mezzanine balcony

opposite above Detail of the muted tones cast by the angled skylight in the living-dining area

opposite below A bathroom opening off the curving corridor

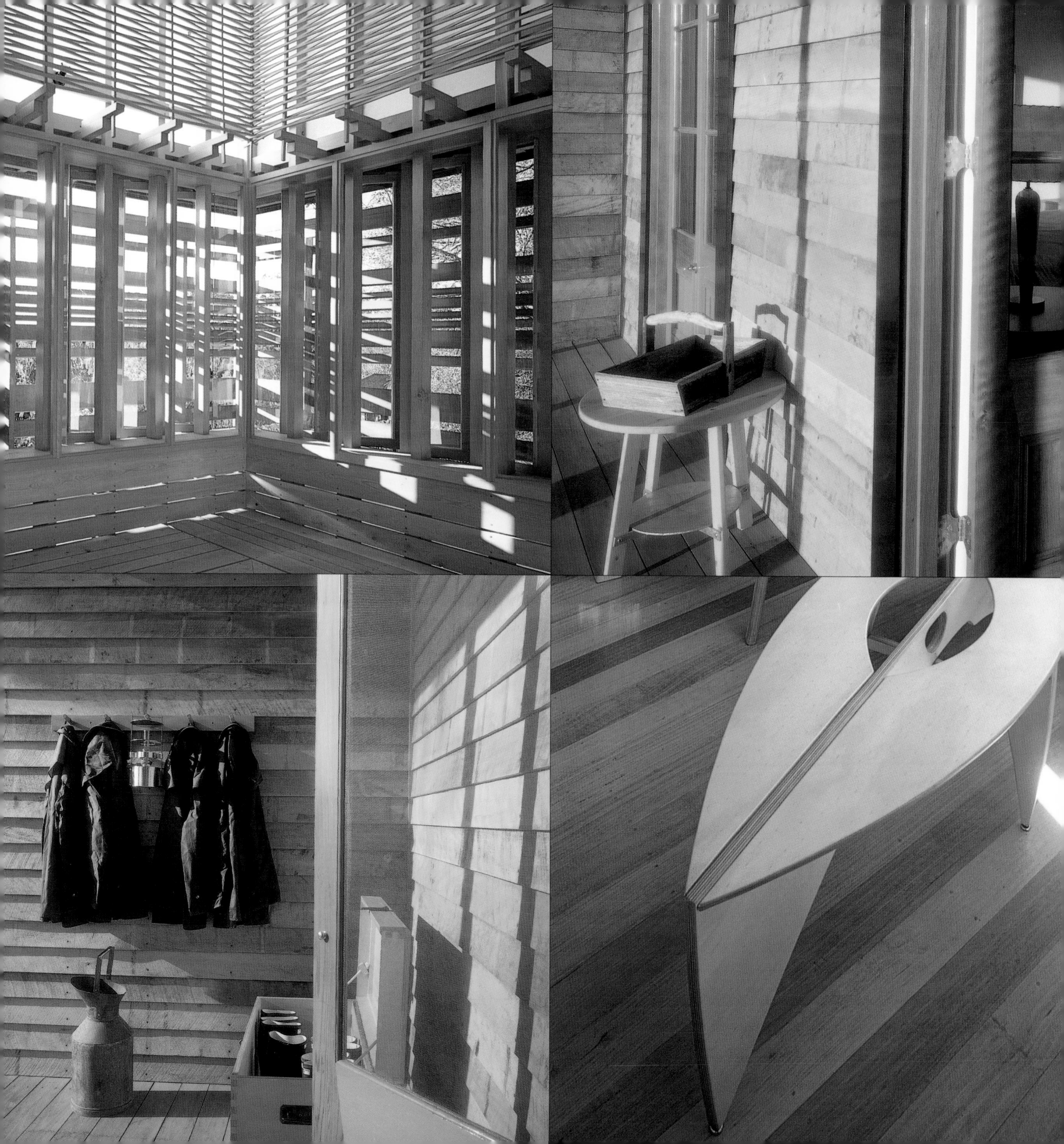

Beverley Garlick's country retreat at Bullio, New South Wales

BUSH

Sherbrooke Forest, Victoria

BUSH

Bushland is never far from Australian cities, many of which are situated on the edge of forested hinterlands. Sydney, for example, is surrounded by national parks, including the profusely forested ranges of the Blue Mountains. Much of this wilderness is easily accessible to urban populations and bush houses are often no more than an hour or two from busy city centres. Although beach houses may be the preferred destination for Australians when taking their annual holidays, bush houses make ideal weekend retreats. Because of the proximity of bushlands to crowded cities, some bush houses serve as principal residences, with the occupants commuting daily. Whether they are used throughout the year or only at weekends, bush houses reflect the yearnings of a sophisticated urban population for a simpler and more rustic environment, albeit one with all the amenities of city life.

On the whole, the bush houses included here are a far cry from the working stations of farmers and graziers (except for the outback station at Burrawang in New South Wales and the sheep farm at Kyneton north of Melbourne). Even so, these dwellings possess many genuine bush characteristics. One of the accomplishments of the current generation of designers has been the creation of a new rural idiom. As already noted, this is derived from the corrugated tin shed that once lurked at the back of every country property. This rudimentary metallic prototype has inspired a broad range of adaptations, most of which are easily reconciled with the modernist tradition. The layout of such houses tends to be simple, with central living-dining-kitchen areas opening directly onto decks with uninterrupted landscape views. These open plans are very similar to the modernist designs in Australia from the mid-century onwards. While there is no claim here that the new bush houses should be categorized as modernist, they nevertheless display the same straightforward planning, low elevational profiles and unfussy detailing, only here these ideals tend to be realized in metal.

While all of the bush houses in this book manifest these attributes in one way or another, Rick Bzowy's project in the Adelaide Hills may be taken as typical. Tucked into a sloping wooded site, this modest weekender is little more than a double-height living space, with a pair of bedrooms and a study occupying a narrow mezzanine. The exterior gleams with aluminium louvres that shield the fully glazed north wall, while on the south side a gently curved, corrugated tin wall sweeps up to meet the roof cladding, itself slightly curved. This contrast of curving surfaces lends an aesthetic distinction to what is otherwise a basic bush shed. In his double-shed house at Mount Wilson, hidden in the dense forest west of Sydney, the architect Glenn Murcutt never loses sight of the archetype. Two sheds, one for living, the other for a pottery studio, are elegantly counterpoised at either end of a rectangular pool.

Further variants of this model are to be found throughout the country. Beverley Garlick roofs each of the shed-like structures of her country retreat at Bullio in outback New South Wales with a 'barrel vault' of galvanized iron. Inside, the curving roofs are lined with curving plywood panels, providing a welcome, warm-toned contrast to the metal. As in so many other bush houses, the end walls open up to offer vast, unimpeded vistas of the surrounding countryside. A more complex scheme is devised by Lindsay Holland at Dewhurst, an hour east of Melbourne. The three shed-like wings of this homestead are laid out in U-shaped formation, each roofed with a combination of curved and angled sheet-iron meeting at the gutters. Additional sheets serve as wall cladding to give the house its overall metallic appearance.

A radical rethinking of the bush shed prototype is evident in Grose Bradley's house at Balgownie. The structural

Rick Bzowy's house in the Adelaide Hills, South Australia

Sheep near Horsham, Victoria

Iron ore country in Western Australia

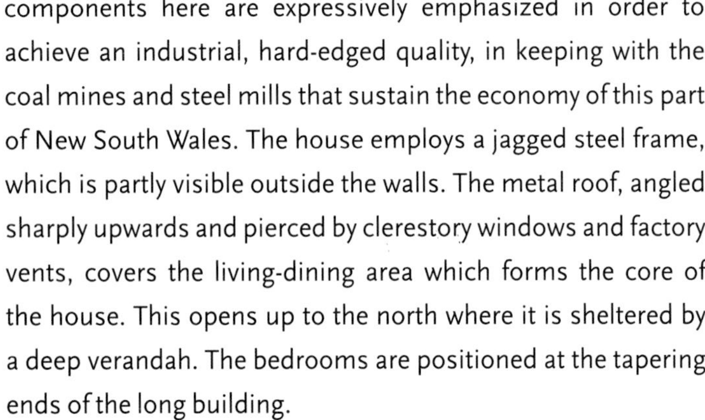

components here are expressively emphasized in order to achieve an industrial, hard-edged quality, in keeping with the coal mines and steel mills that sustain the economy of this part of New South Wales. The house employs a jagged steel frame, which is partly visible outside the walls. The metal roof, angled sharply upwards and pierced by clerestory windows and factory vents, covers the living-dining area which forms the core of the house. This opens up to the north where it is sheltered by a deep verandah. The bedrooms are positioned at the tapering ends of the long building.

Queensland architects show particular virtuosity in their handling of the metallic bush house. In their modest hilltop pavilion at Pomona, Lindsay and Kerry Clare strip down the tin-shed paradigm to its essential components. The house is little more than a steel-framed hut, with a broad gable supported on angled struts. The interior wraps around a sleeping zone which is separated by wooden louvres from the central living-dining area. At nearby Kenilworth, John Mainwaring has restored a traditional Queenslander and added a shed-like wing with spacious suites of rooms on two levels. The new structure is clad in a combination of metal sheeting and painted fibro-cement panels to create multi-textured, colouristic façades. So that the inhabitants might be reminded of the metallic prototype that inspired this addition, one wall is cloaked in uncut corrugated tin sheets ending in an audacious jagged profile.

Gabriel Poole's own triple-shed house near Lake Weyba achieves spatial complexity in a deceptively simple way. Here the original tin shed is respected, but multiplied to create a sequence of three detached, sloping roofed structures. Daylight is controlled by rolling metallic blinds on the northern aspect of the principal living-dining shed-like wing of the house, and elsewhere by pivoting panels and shuttered openings. Each wing has translucent vinyl sheets suspended over the angled girders, giving the interiors a dappled visual quality that perfectly complements the lightly wooded landscape in which the house stands.

The wooded hinterland that lies an hour north of Sydney offers a perfect setting for another series of bush houses.

The Olgas, Northern Territory

Ferns on the banks of a fast-flowing stream, Victoria

Luigi Rosselli's estuary house at Cottage Point contrasts finely chiselled masonry with delicately worked timbers to achieve a fluid elegance, sustained in the boat-shaped decks that project outwards into the treetops. Peter Stuchbury's forest cabin at nearby Clareville presents a complete contrast, having been designed for and partly built by a client intent on natural living. Superimposed living-cooking and sleeping zones are linked by a ladder, with a deck for outdoor dining extending into the forest from the lower level. The house is intentionally rustic in its finish, with an exposed steel frame, sliding wooden shutters and infill fibro panels. This simplest of dwellings is covered with a curved roof of corrugated iron that seems to float above the bedroom. A related weekend house by Grose Bradley in a similarly secluded site in the Adelaide Hills encases the principal living-dining area in a curving but tapering mass of solid mud-brick pierced by deeply set windows. The metallic element here is reduced to a tin canopy carried on sloping rods.

The notion of the bush house as a substantial residence finds its ultimate expression in a monumental, somewhat severe project overlooking a vineyard in the Yarra valley, northeast of Melbourne. Here Allan Powell creates a Mediterranean-style villa encased in solid masonry, relieved only by occasional slender stainless steel rods. The interior is not intended for informal living but for grand entertainment, as is clear from the handsome proportions of the dining and living areas and the impressive art collection that lines the walls. Another substantial reworking of the bush house is the extensive sheep farm at nearby Kyneton. The residential wing of this project is overshadowed by an imposing and symmetrically planned concrete-lined court, off which open the workshop and shearing shed. A small slanting doorway in the rear concrete wall leads to the residential wing. This is conceived as a glazed shed, complete with an angled corrugated roof cantilevering dramatically outwards. Despite the use of elaborate metallic surfaces, the plan reverts to a simple open scheme with living-dining in the middle and bedrooms at either end. Once again the archetypal bush shed has been revived and recast, only to surface in radical, late modernist garb.

HOMESTEAD ADDITION, KENILWORTH, QUEENSLAND

the queenslander, old and new

Built for a European client who spends part of each year in Queensland, this sprawling residence in the hilly hinterland of the Sunshine Coast incorporates a restored late nineteenth-century homestead with a raised living area surrounded by a screened verandah. A covered gallery leads from here to the new wing which accommodates the kitchen-dining area as well as the master bedroom. The use of corrugated iron cladding, both for the walls and the roof, as well as painted fibro panels and slatted timbers, helps to integrate new with old. The result is a fresh interpretation of the traditional Queenslander.

opposite above The new wing, showing the original house to the right

opposite below Verandahs opening off the new wing are shaded by corrugated iron and timber slats

right The new wing is faced on one side with sheets of corrugated iron ending in a jagged metallic profile

below The dining room in the old wing can be segregated by sliding timber-louvred panels

left The restored living area in the original house, roofed with a gabled ceiling, opens up on all sides

above The restored verandah, with fly-wire screens, surrounds the glazed dining room

metallic curves

Designed by the architect Peter Elliott, this house is set in wooded sheep-grazing country near Horsham in western Victoria. The simple shed-like layout of the building is modified by slender steel supports which carry the corrugated iron roof well beyond the steel and glass walls. The gently curving roof gives the exterior a bold profile reminiscent of an aircraft hangar.

left Water storage tanks at the rear of the house are integrated into the overall metal fabric

opposite Corrugated iron panels at the front of the house create a formal entrance to the glazed living area

below Louvred windows light the living-dining area which is finished with whitewashed panels set between the supporting trusses of the metallic frame

DOUBLE-WING HOUSE, MARGARET RIVER, WESTERN AUSTRALIA

textural contrasts

This project forms part of an extensive residential estate laid out in grazing country some three hours north of Perth. The house comprises two clearly articulated wings separated by an internal corridor lined with plywood panels. The flat-roofed living-dining-kitchen area, which faces north, is glazed on three sides, with timber decks at either end. The bedroom-bathroom wing on the south has a distinctive gabled roof which appears to float above the supporting mud-brick walls.

left The gabled end of the bedroom wing, next to which is an open deck enclosed by concrete walls

opposite Sleekly finished woodwork in the master bedroom

below The principal living-dining area incorporates a small interior court with sliding glass doors

traditional homestead

This fully working estate was designed by Denton Corker Marshall for a Japanese client intent upon re-creating a traditional Australian homestead. The revivalist spirit of the architecture is modified by a preference for clean lines that reflects a contemporary concern for geometry and line. The estate consists of residential and service buildings spread over some 4,000 hectares of grazing land on the edge of state-protected forest in outback New South Wales. The sustained use of finely worked timberwork, both for exterior cladding and varnished interior finishes, gives the homestead the highest aesthetic appeal. Its luxurious interior contrasts with the simple form of the exterior.

opposite far left Employees at Burrawang live in a rudimentary gabled building with deeply set verandahs and window openings

opposite above The principal residence is flanked by accommodation for employees

opposite below Panelled glass doors define the axial corridor leading through the principal residence to the living area

above A centrally placed hearth is the focus for the living area, with functional farm implements used as a wall display

HILLTOP PAVILION, POMONA, QUEENSLAND

lightweight and small-scaled

Lindsay and Kerry Clare designed this house for a retired couple who wished to enjoy the distant panorama of Queensland's Glasshouse Mountains from their inland hilltop site at Pomona. A simple, small-scale pavilion, raised above grassy terrain and roofed with a simple gable with generous overhangs, is built of plywood panels with glass louvres set into a lightweight steel frame. In spite of its diminutive scale, the interior is surprisingly spacious, with the principal living-dining area wrapped around the slatted bedroom area.

opposite The dining and living areas open off the deck

left The house as seen through the carport with its sharply angled roof

below The slatted wooden panels of the bedroom

ecologically aware and environmentally sound

Grose Bradley's house, tucked into the forested hills some twenty kilometres east of Adelaide, is an ecologically conscious project which uses solar power and employs a recycling toilet. The house consists of a traditionally built, mud-brick core, deeply punctuated by openings which reveal the tapering mass of the masonry. Laid out with two walls at right angles joined by a sweeping curve, the house is roofed by an angled canopy of corrugated iron, partly supported by a slender steel pipe.

left Steps ascend to the bedroom mezzanine through which run the painted steel tubes that anchor the roof

opposite The modest scale of the house, with its mud-brick and metallic textures, blends effortlessly into the landscape

below The full-height living space is an essay in diverse wooden textures, from the panelled floor to the smooth cladding of the ceiling that overhangs the kitchen zone

metallic inside and out

Nestling in the wooded hills of the Dandenong ranges an hour east of Melbourne, this house is associated with an active plant nursery. Three separate wings are arranged in U-shaped formation, each roofed with an inverted gable of corrugated iron and joined to the walls by a gentle arc of the same metal. The principal rectangular wing has living, dining and cooking areas in the middle, with bedroom and study at the ends, all opening onto a continuous, generously shaded verandah. One of the other wings accommodates guest rooms, bathroom and laundry.

opposite The living area is enclosed by bookcases and room-dividers, with the bedroom beyond

left A storage tank at the end of the main wing collects rainwater from the central roof gutter

below A wood-burning stove provides the focal point for the study

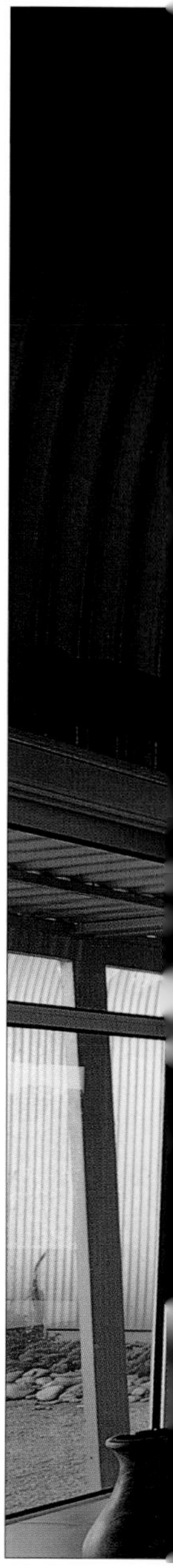

opposite above View of the main wing showing the side verandah opening off the living-dining space, and the rainwater storage tank at the end

opposite below A glimpse of the bedroom from the living area

below The corrugated metallic ceiling runs without interruption through the whole length of the house

forest idyll

Glenn Murcutt designed this double-shed house for a retired academic whose wife is a potter. The residential wing comprises a core living area with kitchen-dining space and a guest bedroom at one end, and the master bedroom at the other. The interior is lit by louvred glass panels, and has a gently curved ceiling which is echoed in the corrugated iron roof. The house is approached by a bridge-like walkway that runs along the side of a long, rectangular pool. A second, smaller shed structure at the other end of the pool accommodates the pottery studio and garage.

opposite above and below Sliding glass panels allow the living area to open out to the landscape. Shade is provided by a roof extension carried on slender angled struts that mimic the branches of nearby trees

right Looking out from the pottery studio across the pool to the main residential wing

below The central living space with furniture arranged around the wood-burning stove

TRIPLE-SHED HOUSE, LAKE WEYBA, QUEENSLAND

queensland vernacular

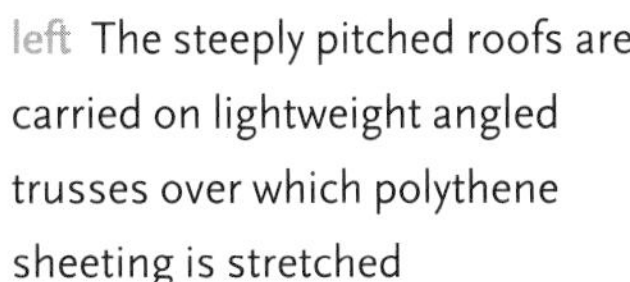

left The steeply pitched roofs are carried on lightweight angled trusses over which polythene sheeting is stretched

Gabriel Poole, an architect, and his wife Elizabeth, an artist, designed this residence in the hinterland of Queensland's Sunshine Coast for themselves. Three lightweight sheds standing in a row, each facing the back of the other, separately accommodate living zones, dining and study areas, washing and bathing spaces, and sleeping area. The sheds, linked by an open walkway flanked by water storage tanks, are built of lightweight metallic frames, partly clad in galvanized steel sheeting, with glazing and openable plywood flaps.

opposite The trio of sheds set in the low open forest that fringes Lake Weyba

left A painted twig sculpture by Elizabeth Poole forms part of the natural environment

opposite left The bedroom in the third and smallest shed at the rear

opposite below The living area in the first shed as seen from the verandah that runs along the front of the house

below A spa bath in the second shed where all bathing and washing areas are located

treetop living

Originally designed for professional musicians, this magnificently sited house by Luigi Rosselli enjoys matchless views of the densely wooded estuary of the Hawkesbury river, just an hour north of Sydney. Its roughly finished sandstone walls, topped with timber-clad pavilions, blend seamlessly into the surrounding eucalyptus trees.

opposite The main living block, surrounded by a verandah, has beautiful views over the Hawkesbury river

above The nautically inspired front deck, projecting through the trees, appears to be suspended over the river

opposite far left Curving decks with graceful railings connect the different zones of the house

opposite above The upper deck leads to the timber-clad music studio, seemingly isolated in the forest

opposite below A timber bridge leads to the entrance hall, roofed with a circular copper-clad roof which curves gently outwards

above The bathroom is luxuriously appointed, with cherrywood cabinets and a mosaic-lined tub

SHEEP FARM, KYNETON, VICTORIA

rural industrial

Denton Corker Marshall's farm nestling in open grazing country near Kyneton, north of Melbourne, comprises a residence, guest wing, workshop and shearing shed grouped around three sides of a court. A narrow doorway in the middle of the rear wall of the court leads to the house. Built mainly of metal and glass, the design conforms to the traditional shed layout, with a single internal space given over to living, cooking and dining, and bedrooms and bathrooms at both ends.

above The central kitchen space gives onto a verandah that runs the full length of the house

left The handbasin in the bathroom appears to float in front of a glass wall

opposite above The entrance court to the farm is surrounded by a formidable barrier of precast concrete walls

opposite centre Galvanized iron sheets line the undersides of the angled canopies that shelter the main wing of the house and the open corridor which separates the house from the walled court

opposite below In the bedroom, low, slit windows offer views of the landscape from the bed

above The narrow, slanting entrance to the house in the centre of the rear wall of the court

JAGGED FRAME HOUSE, BALGOWNIE, NEW SOUTH WALES

steel style

Conceived in the spirit of the steel mills of nearby Wollongong in coastal New South Wales, this house is entirely clad in corrugated galvanized panels. The architects Grose Bradley employ a jagged framework that is fully expressed on the interior and partly on the exterior where it protrudes beyond the tapering ends of the building. The framework contains a central living-dining area that opens onto the shaded verandah; bedroom and study are accommodated at either end.

top The house is suspended over gravel in the middle of a well-tended garden with its outer cladding tucked into the supporting jagged frame

above The kitchen is sited in an extension to one side

above Steps ascend to the verandah that runs the full length of the living-dining area

right The central living-dining area has clerestory windows and industrial vents

below The house is entered across a bridge that passes by a service tower

mediterranean formality

Commissioned by a well-known restaurant owner, this hilltop villa an hour north of Melbourne is associated with a working vineyard. The architect Allan Powell designed this solidly built, concrete house in a Mediterranean manner, with a sequence of spaces opening one into another. Identically sized rooms on the north side accommodate living, dining and cooking areas and an office, each opening onto a terrace. The south side is given over to a gallery running the full length of the house, intended for displaying art and entertaining on a grand scale. The gallery looks out onto a courtyard planted with plane trees.

above Rows of plane trees and a meditation pool in the courtyard

opposite above left High walls surround the courtyard on three sides, offering protection from the wind

opposite above right A galvanized frame lightens the austere northern aspect of the house

opposite below The dining room with its large fireplace flanked by piles of neatly stacked firewood

prefabricated and self-sufficient

Designed by Beverley Garlick for a professional female client based in Sydney, this house at Bullio near Mittagong in rural New South Wales consists of three shed-like pavilions roofed with 'barrel vaults' of brightly painted corrugated iron. The main wing, which is devoted to living, dining and cooking, is linked to a second smaller wing comprising a suite of two bedrooms. The third detached wing serves as a store and garage. The remoteness of the site meant that the buildings had to be prefabricated; it was also essential that they be self-sufficient in terms of water and power.

opposite Windows at either side of the plywood-clad living space look out over the landscape

right The residential wing is entered through a porch sheltered by a 'barrel vault' of corrugated iron

below The three shed-like wings of the house are grouped in a grassy valley beneath a forested ridge

FOREST CABIN, CLAREVILLE, NEW SOUTH WALES

a home for natural living

Tucked away in the forested hinterland of Pittwater, an hour north of Sydney, this miniature, low-cost house consists of two superimposed chambers, with living and cooking beneath, and sleeping above. Outdoor dining takes place on an extended deck protected by a canopy. Mostly constructed by the client and his architect Peter Stuchbury, the house has an elementary steel frame that supports an arc of corrugated iron. Sliding windows and wooden panels give the interior an unusual lightness and transparency.

left Steps ascending to the bedroom

above The deck in front of the house is shaded from the sun by an orange canopy, a vivid flash of colour contrasting with the green bush

left The bedroom on the upper level is surrounded by windows upon which the roof seems to float

below The living-cooking space opens up at either side by means of sliding panels

STYLE AND SHOPPING DIRECTORY

furniture, lighting, fabrics, kitchenware, bathroom accessories

SYDNEY

Anibou
726 Bourke Road, Redfern 2016
(02) 9319 0655

Australian Living
corner Glebe Point and Broadway,
Glebe 2037
(02) 9518 8288

Camargue
Shop 6, 914 Military Road, Mosman 2088
(02) 9960 6234

Dinosaur Designs
339 Oxford Street, Paddington 2021
(02) 9361 3776

77 Strand Arcade, Sydney 2000
(02) 9223 2953

ECC Lighting
36 Gosbell Street, Paddington 2021
(02) 9380 7922

Echo Echo
211 Bourke Street, East Sydney 2000
(02) 9361 6699

Empire Homewares
18–20 Oxford Street, Paddington 2021
(02) 9380 8877

Inne
47 Queen Street, Woollahra 2025
(02) 9362 9900

Papaya Studio
15b Transvaal Avenue, Double Bay 2028
(02) 9362 1620

West Eight Furniture
corner Bourke and Cathedral Streets,
Woolloomooloo 2011
(02) 9326 9877

White
785 Military Road, Mosman 2088
(02) 9968 4559

MELBOURNE

Archaeos
16–26 George Street, Fitzroy 3065
(03) 9417 3588

Cochrane & Galloway
176 Burwood Road, Hawthorn 3122
(03) 9818 3300

Colours of Provence
546 Burwood Road, Hawthorn 3122
(03) 9819 1922

Dinosaur Designs
562 Chapel Street, South Yarra 3141
(03) 9827 2600

Egg
96–98 Church Street, Brighton 3186
(03) 9593 3400

Hermon & Hermon Plus
556 Swan Street, Richmond 3121
(03) 9427 0599

Husk
557 Malvern Road, Toorak 3142
(03) 9827 2700

Kazari
290 Malvern Road, Prahran 3181
(03) 9521 1107

Marco Fabrics
155 Auburn Road, Hawthorn 3122
(03) 9882 7238

Minimax
582 Burke Road, Camberwell, 3124
(03) 9813 0888

585 Malvern Road, Toorak 3142
(03) 9826 0022

Mondo Furniture
5 Alexander Drive, Burwood 3125
(03) 9888 7945

Space Furniture
310 Toorak Road, South Yarra 3141
(03) 9824 1300

BRISBANE

Corso de' Fiori
46 Douglas Street, Milton 4064
(07) 3369 7122

De De Ce
124 Petrie Terrace, Brisbane 4000
(07) 3367 0755

PERTH

Katsui Design
343 Stirling Highway, Claremont 6010
(08) 9385 3005

Old Empire
121 Hay Street, Subiaco 6008
(08) 9388 1318

Proportions
853 Wellington Street, West Perth 6005
(08) 9226 2626

ADELAIDE

Now Furniture
45 Gilbert Street,
Adelaide 5000
(08) 823 18377

CANBERRA

Flair Furniture
8 Ipswich Street,
Fyshwick 2609
(02) 623 91169

INDEX OF ARCHITECTS AND DESIGNERS

Neil Durbach and Camilla Block
Level 3, 441 Kent Street
Sydney 2000
(02) 9261 3951
PROJECTS
Rushcutters Bay, Sydney: angled wing house 98–99
Surry Hills, Sydney: rooftop apartment 24, 46–47

Edmond and Corrigan
46 Little Latrobe Street
Melbourne 3000
(03) 9662 2651
PROJECTS
Seaton Cove, Tasmania: weatherboard house 112–113, 140–141

Peter Elliott
2/290 Latrobe Street
Melbourne 3000
(03) 9329 8277
PROJECTS
Horsham, Victoria: hangar house 166–167

Engelen Moore
62–64 Sophia Street
Surry Hills, New South Wales 2010
(02) 9281 0372
PROJECTS
Neutral Bay, Sydney: house with sawtooth lights 12, 66, 74–75
Redfern, Sydney: studio residence 12, 23–24, 30–31

Beverley Garlick
135 Catherine Street
Leichardt, New South Wales 2040
(02) 9569 8205
PROJECTS
Bullio, New South Wales: country retreat 16, 156–157, 159, 196–197

Sean Godsell
34 Queens Road
Melbourne 3000
(03) 9820 0999
PROJECTS
Kew, Melbourne: architect's residence 12, 67, 76–77

Grose Bradley
Bligh Voller Neiled Pty Ltd
Level 2, 189 Kent Street
Sydney 2000
(02) 9252 1222
PROJECTS
Adelaide Hills, South Australia: weekend house 16, 161, 174–175
Balgownie, New South Wales: jagged frame house 16, 159–160, 192–193

Kerry Hill
30 Mouat Street
Fremantle, Western Australia 6160
(03) 9336 4545
PROJECTS
Margaret River, Western Australia: double-wing house 168–169

Lindsay Holland
5/289 Flinders Lane
Melbourne 3000
(03) 9650 3744
PROJECTS
Dewhurst, Victoria: U-shaped house 16, 159, 176–179

Dale Jones-Evans
Loft 5, 96 Albion Street
Surry Hills, New South Wales 2010
(02) 9211 0626
PROJECTS
Hawthorn, Melbourne: postmodern dwelling 15, 66, 88–89

Nonda Katsalidis
Nation Fender Katsalidis Architects
Level 1, 388 Lonsdale Street
Melbourne 3000
(03) 9600 1299
PROJECTS
Melbourne: apartment block 24, 50–51
Melbourne: duplex 32–33
Richmond, Melbourne: silo apartments 23, 42–43
St Andrews Beach, Victoria: oceanside bunker 15, 111–112, 126–127
St Kilda, Melbourne: apartments 67

Tom Kovac
1/422 Queen Street,
Melbourne 3000
(03) 9329 4880
PROJECTS
Darlinghurst, Sydney: Tonic restaurant 15
Hawthorn, Melbourne: whitewashed moulded house 15, 65, 78–79

Ed Lippmann
570 Crown Street
Surry Hills, New South Wales 2010
(02) 9318 0844
PROJECTS
Mosman, Sydney: house 12, 67

Geoff Lovie
Heather Buttrose Associates
Office 1, Cowper Wharf Road
Woolloomoolloo, New South Wales 2011
(02) 9368 1748
PROJECTS
Queanbeyan, New South Wales: timber-clad house 15, 65, 92–93

Peter Maddison
1st floor, 98 Bank Street
South Melbourne 3205
(03) 9696 3636
PROJECTS
Phillip Island, Victoria: towered cabin 17, 111, 128–129

INDEX OF ARCHITECTS AND DESIGNERS

INDEX OF PLACES

Peter Stuchbury
Stuchbury & Pape Architects
Studio 4, 364 Barrenjoey Road
Newport, New South Wales 2106
(02) 9979 5030
PROJECTS
Clareville, New South Wales: forest cabin 17, 161, 198–199

Anthony Styant-Browne
6A Montrose Street
Hawthorn East, Victoria 3123
(03) 9813 3466
PROJECTS
North Melbourne, Melbourne: warehouse conversion 6

Nick Tridente
203 Melbourne Street
North Adelaide, South Australia 5006
(08) 8267 3922
PROJECTS
North Haven, South Australia: wooden-frame house 111, 130–131

Alexander Tzannes
63 Myrtle Street
Chippendale, New South Wales 2008
(02) 9319 3744
PROJECTS
Bellevue Hill, Sydney: masonry villa 66, 94–95

John Wardle
25 William Street
Richmond, Victoria 3121
(03) 9421 0700
PROJECTS
Balnarring, Victoria: plywood house 111, 142–145

Wood Marsh
466 William Street
West Melbourne, Victoria 3003
(03) 9329 4920
PROJECTS
Caulfield, Victoria: family villa 15, 66, 96–97

ACKNOWLEDGMENTS

Throughout our work on this book, we have depended both on the cooperation of the designers and architects featured to provide essential information and to arrange introductions, and the indulgence of the householders who tolerated the bothersome intrusion of photo shoots. Among those who received us with particular hospitality were Peter and Julie Bowen, Ross and Elizabeth Chisholm, Charles and Cheryl Hammond, Ken Israel, Chester and Sue Keon-Cohen, Barrie and Raine Marshall, Paul and Janet Newman, Andrew and Jane Norbury, Geelum Simpson and Sheila Lee, and Daniel Thomas.

A number of friends and colleagues provided much-needed advice in the planning and execution of the project. They include Brit Andresen and Peter O'Gorman, Haig Beck and Jackie Cooper, David Brand and Fooi-ling Khoo, Ross Feller, Phillip Goad, Davina Jackson, Graham Jahn, Ian McKay, David Pidgeon, Neville Quarry and Jo Wodak. George Michell would like to thank the Faculty of Architecture, Building and Planning at the University of Melbourne for a supporting travel grant. John Gollings is grateful to Reiner Blunck and Trevor Mein for permitting their photographs to appear in this book (see pp. 136–137 and pp. 128–129 respectively).

Without the untiring patience and expert managerial skills of Sue Shanahan at the Gollings studio it is unlikely that this project could ever have been undertaken, let alone completed. Anne Engel has been a constant source of encouragement. To all these individuals we extend our grateful thanks.

John Gollings and George Michell